CAMBRIA COUNTY PIONEERS:
A COLLECTION OF BRIEF BIOGRAPHICAL AND OTHER SKETCHES RELATING TO THE EARLY HISTORY OF CAMBRIA COUNTY, PENNSYLVANIA

JAMES M. SWANK

HERITAGE BOOKS
2008

HERITAGE BOOKS
AN IMPRINT OF HERITAGE BOOKS, INC.

Books, CDs, and more—Worldwide

For our listing of thousands of titles see our website
at
www.HeritageBooks.com

Published 2008 by
HERITAGE BOOKS, INC.
Publishing Division
100 Railroad Ave. #104
Westminster, Maryland 21157

International Standard Book Numbers
Paperbound: 978-0-7884-0890-8
Clothbound: 978-0-7884-7077-6

THE FIRST PRESBYTERIAN CHURCH IN JOHNSTOWN.
BUILT 1835. TORN DOWN 1863.

HON. CYRUS L. PERSHING.

CONTENTS.

PREFACE.

At the outset I wish my friends who read this volume to understand plainly that it is not the result of a deliberate purpose to write a book of more or less historical value. It is a compilation entirely, with two exceptions, of twenty biographical and other sketches relating to Cambria county that were written years ago, some of them many years ago. It has fallen to my lot to prepare from time to time and publish biographical sketches of some of the prominent men of Cambria county in the old days, a few of whom were then living but most of whom had passed to the other side, and these sketches, now reproduced, occupy the larger part of the following pages; the remainder of the volume is devoted to subjects of historical interest relating to pioneer days in Cambria county which I have had occasion to consider in years gone by. The names and the work of the pioneers of any community should never be forgotten. Of the biographical sketches three relate to old and prominent citizens of Cambria county who have died in Philadelphia and with whom my old acquaintance had been renewed.

I have compiled these sketches not only to preserve the memory of prominent and worthy citizens of Cambria county who have had much to do with its early history but also to preserve many historical facts of local interest which otherwise might be wholly lost, some of which are interwoven with those of a purely personal character. That Johnstown was a shipping point of importance on the Conemaugh long before the Pennsylvania Canal or the Pennsylvania Railroad was ever dreamed of; that there were many iron enterprises at and near Johnstown before the Cambria Iron Works were built; that an Ebensburg man was the private secretary of Governor Curtin during the civil war; that the editor of a Johnstown newspaper was in the battle of San Jacinto in 1836; that more than sixty years ago there was a volunteer military company at Summerhill called the Quitman Guards; that a citizen of Johnstown was the chairman of the executive committee of the Centennial Commission, and that other citizens of Johnstown have occupied high official positions; that there was no post office at Johnstown until 1811; that there were great floods in Johnstown in the early days—all these and many more facts of strictly historical value relating to the early days of Cambria county are certainly worthy of preservation.

The attention of the reader is called to the date of publication of each sketch, which will be found immediately under its title. I could not rewrite the sketches to adapt them to present conditions. They are reprinted substantially as they were originally written. If any errors of fact should be discovered I can only plead in explanation that all but one of the sketches were written away from my old home in the mountains.

PHILADELPHIA, December 26, 1910.   J. M. S.

CAMBRIA COUNTY PIONEERS.

THE FOUNDING OF THE JOHNSTOWN TRIBUNE.

WRITTEN IN SEPTEMBER, 1882, AND PUBLISHED IN THE JOHNSTOWN DAILY AND WEEKLY TRIBUNE.

THE main line of the Pennsylvania Railroad from Philadelphia to Pittsburgh, with its leased connections, was completed to the latter city late in 1852. On the 10th of December of that year cars were run through from Philadelphia to Pittsburgh for the first time. The construction of this great thoroughfare led to the development of extensive mining and manufacturing enterprises in many parts of Pennsylvania, and particularly in the western part. In the spring of 1853 the first spadeful of earth was removed at Johnstown to prepare for the foundations of the Cambria Iron Works, and on July 27, 1854, these works went into operation. Before they had made their first rail, however, or had turned a single wheel, the writer of these lines, inspired perhaps by the hope of better days for Johnstown, but most likely ruled by a destiny which he did not understand, issued on the 7th day of December, 1853, the first number of the *Cambria Tribune*, an enterprise worthy to be referred to on the same page, we trust, with the two more extensive enterprises already mentioned. We know, at least, that it had just as worthy an origin. But it had a very humble origin, and, unlike the man who gets up in the world and unwisely forgets the days of his poverty and dependence, we propose to-day to take the old friends and the new friends of the *Tribune* into our confidence and tell them how the little newspaper got its start.

There had been published in Cambria county since about 1825, sometimes at Johnstown and sometimes at Ebensburg, a Whig newspaper which had in turn many owners and many names. The first copy of this paper which we have seen was styled the *Cambria Gazette* and was printed at Ebensburg in 1827. Subsequently it was called *The Sky* and afterwards again the *Cambria Gazette.* While bearing this last name the press and fixtures of the office found their final resting place in Johnstown. But while they became stationary the name of the paper did not have the same good fortune, nor did the paper's ill-luck of having frequent changes of ownership come to an end. Finally, in the summer of 1853, one of those episodes in its history occurred which had frequently occurred before—the paper came to a dead stop.

It was under such circumstances as these that the press and fixtures of the office—subscription list and good will were of little value—came into my hands in November, 1853, with an understanding with a few prominent Whigs of the town, in whose custody I found the press and fixtures, that I was to publish a Whig newspaper if I could but that they were not to be responsible for my debts if I failed. With this encouragement, such as it was, I resolved to go ahead. I had not one dollar of capital but I had that which is better than capital, I had friends, and from them I borrowed about $150. With this money a new dress of long primer type was purchased and also a few bundles of paper. I found the office in a large room on Main street, on the first floor of a frame addition to the Mansion House. The room was unsuitable for a printing office, being low in height, poorly lighted with eight-by-ten glass, uneven upon the floor, and hugging the ground so closely that it was necessary to step down from the sidewalk to get into it. In the rear was the fragrant stableyard of the Mansion House. I recollect very well that the first thing I did on assuming possession was to have that office scrubbed and whitewashed. My landlord was John Dibert and the rent was $30 a year.

I can not, with equal certainty, recall the names of the printers who helped me to issue the first number of the new paper. I set some of the type for the first number myself, but I will say frankly that I did not set it very fast. My impression is that a young man named Hill from Indiana was the journeyman and that Joseph M. Horton and the present proprietor of the *Tribune* were the office boys, Joe also being the carrier. They all worked in the office during the first winter of the new paper's existence and I think that they worked on the first number. Andrew Jackson Hite also worked on the *Tribune* in its early days. Hite and Horton are dead and are buried among strangers. Joe Horton "finished his trade" in the *Tribune* office and became a rapid and correct compositor. Jack Hite was already an accomplished printer, familiar with all the details of the typographic art. He had taken his first lessons in the art in 1846 from Henry C. Devine, the foreman of the *Democratic Courier*, a journalistic venture of our old friend General James Potts, who was assisted in its editorial management by Major Thomas A. Maguire. Jack had for a fellow-apprentice in the *Courier* office John P. Linton, but John did not remain long at the case. Jack afterwards, and prior to the starting of the *Tribune*, acted for a time as the right-hand man of Captain George N. Smith in the publication at Johnstown of *The Allegheny Mountain Echo*.

When I resolved to try my luck as the editor and publisher of a weekly newspaper in Johnstown I would have been glad to continue the name by which the old paper had longest been known, the *Cambria Gazette*. It was euphonious and appropriate, and, although associated with frequent failures, it had a certain hold upon the affections of the old Whigs of the county, who remembered that it had rejoiced with them when they were victorious and condoled with them when they were defeated. But I was persuaded that persistence in the use of the name would be ominous of further disaster, and I reluctantly abandoned it and substituted the *Cambria Tribune*. This name I afterwards changed, for obvious reasons, to *The Johnstown Tribune*. I was at the time the *Tribune* was started an admirer of Horace Greeley, whose paper, the *New York Tribune*, was then, as it long had been, the leading Whig newspaper in the country. After it the *Cambria Tribune* was called. I remember well that that ardent and brilliant young Whig, Abram Kopelin, protested warmly against my choice of a name. He said that Horace Greeley's paper was the organ of the Abolitionists, as well as of the Whigs, and that the paper I proposed to start would also be identified in the public mind with the same treasonable faction, which would never, never do. But I had my way. At that time there were few papers in the country whose publishers dared to call them after the *New York Tribune;* now there are hundreds of *Tribunes.* I have always been satisfied with my choice. My venerable friend Abraham Morrison did not strongly object to it, but hoped that I would call the paper *The People's Advocate.*

Well, we laid the new type for the new paper and I gave the boys plenty of copy. Up went the long rows of shining metal, brightening my eyes and gladdening my heart. And where do you think those rows were ? On brass galleys where type is now placed ? There was not one in the office. Our sticks were emptied on a long wooden galley nailed against the wall near the press. This galley would hold three rows of type, each row containing enough type to make about three columns of the paper. It remained in use for several years. When enough type had been set for one side of the paper it was carried directly from this galley to the bed of the press, a handful at a time. Imposing-stone there was none. When the pages were locked up, and not until then, a proof was taken with the press, slips wide enough to take an impression of two columns being used. Corrections were made on the press, and the printers who read this can imagine how disheartening the work would often be, especially when there would be " doublets " or " outs," and more especially when the corrections would have to be made at night by an imperfect light.

Imperfect light ! What do you suppose that old *Tribune* office was lighted with ? Tallow candles, two for five cents, set in low and narrow candlesticks made of lead to prevent them from tilting over. Many a page of ·the *Tribune* has been corrected with the aid of candles set in these candlesticks. When an accident would happen, and the tallow would make the acquaintance of the type in the form, the poor printer became an object of real pity. His task in making corrections was sufficiently hard before. When composition had to be done at night, and it had to be pretty often, no other candles or candlesticks than those described were used. The candlestick was placed in the " e " box. In those days Johnstown had not been blessed with either gaslight or coal-oil lamps.

When the form for one side of the paper had been made ready, and the press had also been made ready, the hardest work in the office commenced. An edition of about five hundred copies was to be printed, and it invariably took a pressman and a roller-boy the whole of a half day, or from early in the evening until midnight, as the case might be, to print one side of that edition. The same amount of labor was of course required to print the other side.

What sort of a press did we have ? We had a press, reader, which we would gladly put in a glass case if we had it now. But the press is lost ; we really do not know what became of it. It was a two-pull Ramage press—that is, the platen was only large enough to cover one page of our little paper. The bed of the press was run in until the platen covered one page, when the lever was pulled and that page was printed ; then the bed was run in farther until the next page was covered, when it was printed and the bed was run out and the sheet taken off the tympan. It was a hand-press, of course. The operation was like that of printing a paper on a Washington press, except that two pulls were required instead of one. The work of printing even our small edition was exceedingly tedious and very laborious. The press itself was liable, too, to get out of order, and this was an additional drawback. The platen was a smooth-faced wooden block which was attached to the frame by four hooks and many strands of twine. Occasionally a hole would be punched in the face of the platen, the printing of handbills being the most frequent cause of this misfortune, and then the platen had to be untied from the hooks and taken, like a babe in arms, to Thompson R. Kimmell or Napoleon B. Haynes to be planed down until the hole would disappear. We remember nervously standing in front of these cabinet-makers—we generally called on them turn about—and coaxing them to drop all other work until our platen was attended to. When they had kindly given it a smooth face once more we carried it in our arms in triumph back to the office. The exercise of tying it to the hooks then followed. This was a work of no little delicacy, as the tying to the four hooks had to be very evenly done or else one corner of the platen would be sure to drag and the impression of the paper be blurred. The springs which returned the lever to its place, and which also helped to equalize the impression, were made of small pieces of leather.

It will be seen that our press was a very primitive affair. Benjamin Franklin might have worked with it, for it was almost identical in construction, and entirely so in principle, with the one on which he printed *The Pennsylvania Gazette*. We managed to do good work with it, except when something would get wrong with the twine or the bits of leather. Although not on our programme that we should do the presswork for the paper we found that we usually had it to do, editorial dignity counting for nothing when the paper had to come out.

Joe Horton applied the ink with a glue-and-molasses roller. I usually made the rollers myself. I was a fair pressman and a slow but sure compositor but a poor roller-maker. Theoretically I knew how to make a roller, and I always gave the mixture due attention, but often my labor came to naught. The composition would frequently refuse to harden sufficiently and then the work had to be done over again. Many an evening I have stood over the old cannon stove and stirred the mixture until I thought it had been sufficiently cooked, then poured it into the mould and gone home to find in the morning that I had missed it again! I remember, and the present publisher of the *Trib-une* doubtless remembers, a heartbreaking experience in endeavoring to make a roller in a glue-kettle which had little pin-holes in it that let in the water from the other kettle. After several failures, which were attributed first to the molasses and next to the glue, almost every grocery in town being called upon for the former and every drug store for the latter, we finally discovered the cause of the trouble in the pin-holes and I bought a new glue-kettle. Then there was sunshine again and there was a good roller in the *Tribune* office.

Did we ever pi a form in the old *Tribune* office ? We certainly did. It was this way : We did not have twin chases in those days, at least not in the *Tribune* office, and both pages were locked up in one chase. The lifting of so heavy a form to the press required the help, if not all the strength, of two persons. Late one night the present publisher of the *Tribune* assisted me to place the form on its edge on the press and then left it in my hands, trusting me to lay it down properly. I was about to do this when a slip of some kind took place, the form came down all too suddenly, and there was a catastrophe. One page fell out of the form and into a good-sized heap but the other page was safe. We grieve to say that the present publisher of the *Tribune* deserted us that night in our trouble. He left by the front door, with the irreverent remark that we were no printer. We stuck to the wreck alone for several hours ; we were not sleepy enough to go home. In the morning our bad fortune did not look so bad as it did when it happened ; time and patience will cure a printer's trouble as well as nearly all other troubles.

The first number of the *Tribune* made its appearance, as I have said, on the 7th day of December, 1853. Other numbers followed in regular order. I sent the paper to nearly all the householding Whigs in the town and to some Democrats. I also sent it to a few prominent persons at Ebensburg and at other points. But few farmers around Johnstown called to make the acquaintance of the new editor or his paper and I could not send it to their homes ; many of them in those days did not read English. Such farmers, however, as became subscribers for the paper were among its most appreciative readers, and no subscribers were more punctual in paying the printer. After marking off my temporary list the names of those who returned the paper, with the chilling word " refused " marked on its margin, I had about five hundred names left, and it is a singular fact that for several years afterwards the number of subscribers did not materially increase. The Cambria Iron Company failed twice soon after the paper was started and many other adverse circumstances operated against its prosperity. The Whig party was dying, the Democrats were in power in Cambria county, money was scarce, and the times were hard. The same influences which operated against an increase of my subscription list also operated against the receipt of many cash-paying advertisements. Of job work there was not much to do, but what was offered was most thankfully received. Usually advertising is regarded as the life-blood of a country newspaper, but I found in the early days of the *Tribune* that without the job work of the office the paper could not have lived. All jobs were printed on the Ramage press.

The *Tribune* was a four-page paper, six columns to the page. It was exactly one-half as large as the present weekly edition of the *Tribune*. It was large enough, however, for its day. While not what it ought to have been, and might have been under more favorable circumstances, it possessed some characteristics of a meritorious nature that I will be pardoned for referring to. I was my own editor; the young lawyers and the Whig politicians of the town were not called upon, nor would they have been permitted, to help me with their superior editorial skill. The paper appeared regularly on the day of publication, even if we had to work half a night or all night to accomplish this object. The carrier's visits could always be looked for at about the same hour every week. I rarely if ever printed a half sheet, and no matter how serious an accident might happen in our office no edition of the *Tribune* was ever printed in any other office. I made it a rule that advertisements should never appear on the first page of the paper and they never did. I had a department for the farmers on the fourth page and it was rarely omitted. I had but little taste for local news, caring more for general news and general politics; consequently the early volumes of the *Tribune* contain only a brief record of the local events of the day and absolutely none of the gossip of the town. Country newspapers have greatly changed since those days in this particular and I insist have changed for the worse. Better, far better, a bit of poetry, or a scrap of history or biography, or Congressional proceedings than many local items that are now published. I think that if I erred seriously as an editor in those early days it was in devoting too much space

to long selections; the paper was not sufficiently a reflex
of the opinions and temper of the times.

It was hard up-hill work to keep the *Tribune* alive in
its early days. As I have said money was scarce, and I
will add that there was not then one really liberal merchant advertiser in the town. I had good friends among
the merchants, but they did not understand the art of advertising or have much faith in printer's ink. I had no official patronage of any kind. Many of my farmer subscribers, although they paid me promptly, insisted that I must
take "country produce" in lieu of money, and I had to do
it. I have taken from them, on account of their subscriptions, cord-wood, poultry, pumpkins, butter, apples, potatoes,
bacon, blackberries, and even chestnuts. Most of the merchants who advertised with me also insisted that I should
trade out my advertising bills, and I had to do that.

I was often, as may easily be supposed, entirely out of
money, yet I never after the paper was started borrowed a
dollar to keep it going. I made it an inflexible rule that,
when I needed a certain amount of money, I would collect
it if possible from those who owed it to me. If I had not
adopted and adhered to this rule I must have broken down.
My debts, therefore, were always paid when due, and it was
of great service to me that I established the reputation of
being careful in my financial dealings. I was sometimes,
however, most sorely pressed. Upon several occasions when
I needed paper, and did not know where to look for even
$10 to buy it with, I have taken advantage of my posses-
sion of a free pass on the Pennsylvania Railroad and gone
to Pittsburgh to solicit advertisements. I never failed to secure something for my advertising columns, and by making
the price low I could get the cash in advance. With this
I would go to a paper warehouse and buy a few bundles,
or maybe only one bundle. If in immediate need of paper
I have secured the services of a porter to take a bundle to
the Pennsylvania Railroad depot, where I would get the
baggage-master on my return train to carry it to Johnstown. In the evening, or possibly late at night, I would
reach home all right. Better that day's work than to borrow money. Let me add that I have frequently, at the end

of a visit to Pittsburgh, but of course after night, for my
pride was not proof against everything, carried a bundle
of paper on my shoulder from the railroad station to the
Tribune office and wet down a sufficient number of quires
for the next edition.

I need not add to these reminiscenses, which I wish the
reader to understand refer only to the first two years and a
half in the life of the *Tribune*—from 1853 to 1856. My
little enterprise has now grown to be twenty-nine years old,
and it has grown in magnitude and power with its years.
I look upon the fat advertising columns of the large daily
and weekly editions of the paper, and then at the splendid office in which it is printed, as if the transformation
were all a dream. I see advertisements rejected because
there is no room for them; the old *Tribune* had plenty
of room in its advertising columns. I see paper hauled
to the office by the wagon-load and I think of my poor
little bundle. There is a big steam press and there are
other presses in the place of the old Ramage and its
wooden platen. There are tons of type. The proprietor is
not asked to take blackberries and chestnuts in payment
of subscriptions, for the farmers, thanks to the Cambria
Iron Works, are now prosperous and have money in their
pockets. It is all like a dream. But the early days of
the *Tribune*, the hard struggle to give it a start, the disappointments, the heartaches and heartbreaks, the endless
pinching to make both ends meet, the bitter first lessons in
human selfishness—all this is a stern reality which I could
not forget if I would.

My connection with the *Tribune* terminated finally on the last day
of December, 1869. Beginning with the summer of 1856 the paper experienced several changes in management, but in 1864 its sole ownership
and control reverted to my hands, in which they continued until the
December day above mentioned. My entire connection with the *Tribune*
covered a period of about eleven years.

PETER GOUGHNOUR'S REMINISCENCES.

EDITORIAL IN THE JOHNSTOWN TRIBUNE OF SATURDAY, FEBRUARY 9, 1856.

PETER GOUGHNOUR, who was born in Maryland in 1773 and died in Conemaugh township, Cambria county, during the past year, 1855, left a statement of his early recollections of what was in old times called "the Conemaugh country," which statement is now before us. It is much to be regretted that there is not in existence an authentic history of the early settlers and settlements of the Conemaugh country, and with a view to filling a portion of this blank in our annals we will compile from Mr. Goughnour's statement such facts as we think worthy of preservation.

Mr. Goughnour says that the first white settlers in the Conemaugh country were two brothers, Samuel and Solomon Adams. At the time of their settlement, about 1785, the Indians who hunted and fished on the banks and in the waters of the Conemaugh and Stony creek were quite numerous. Samuel Adams lived on Sam's run, about two miles south of the confluence of these two streams, and from him it derived its name. Solomon's cabin was located about midway between the junction of the Conemaugh and Stony creek and his brother's cabin. Solomon's run took its name from him. Samuel Adams and an Indian warrior killed each other with their knives while fighting around a white-oak tree on Sandy run, about five miles east of the junction of the Conemaugh and Stony creek. Their bodies were buried in one grave under the tree.

Mr. Goughnour settled in what is now Conemaugh township in 1798. Cambria county was then a wilderness and not known to geographers. At the date of Mr. Goughnour's settlement the Indians had departed from their Conemaugh hunting grounds, but he says that he had found heaps of stones erected over Indian graves, flint arrows, elk horns, and other relics of their presence. A few of these stone heaps are still standing on the banks of the Stony creek above Johnstown.

Jacob Stutzman, who died in 1816, occupied in 1794 the Conemaugh bottom, now the site of Johnstown, and to which had been given the name of Oldtown. Mr. Stutzman was the first white man who ever occupied the bottom. A son of his was killed by an ox-team which had been scared by a rattlesnake. The body of the boy was buried on the left bank of the Stony creek, where Water street in Kernville is now located.

Joseph Johns, or Schantz, a member of the Amish communion and an industrious and honest man, laid out Conemaugh bottom into town lots in 1800. Those who assisted him to lay out the town, and who became its first citizens, were Peter Goughnour, Joseph Francis, Ludwig Wissinger, and a few others. They named it Conemaugh-town, but it was generally called Johnstown. Mr. Johns died at an advanced age in Conemaugh township, Somerset county.

Dr. Anderson and William Hartley opened the first store in the new town and Isaac Proctor opened the second. The necessaries of life at that time rated very high. Coffee was 50 cents per pound; pepper, allspice, and ginger, 50 cents per pound; shad, 50 cents each; salt, $5 per bushel; wheat, $2 per bushel. All other articles rated accordingly. Wages were from 40 to 50 cents per day.

There were at that time no roads through the wilderness to older settlements and nothing but canoes for navigating the streams. Domestic animals were rare but wild beasts of the forest were quite numerous. Panthers, wolves, bears, etc., prowled at night around the cabins of the pioneers. Nevertheless the first settlers, in Mr. Goughnour's language, had fine times hunting and fishing, as the forest was alive with game and the clear streams were filled with fish. Deer were numerous.

The bottoms in the vicinity of Conemaugh-town were covered with luxuriant verdure and presented a wild and picturesque appearance. The hills also were grand beyond description, with their glorious old forests in which the woodman's axe had never rung. Pea vines, wild sunflowers, grapevines, and other native representatives of the vegetable world twined around and waved between the giant oaks, and spruce, and hickories. What a paradise was that Conemaugh country to its first settlers some fifty years ago !

Still those pioneers had their troubles and those forests and bottoms had their drawbacks. Growing among the tall grass was a noxious weed, resembling garlic in taste and appearance, and called ramps by the settlers, which, when eaten by the cows, was sure to sicken them and put a stop to the supply of milk and butter. The grass, from some cause not stated, did not make good hay, and as the cultivation of corn, oats, rye, etc., was exceedingly limited the result was that in the winter the cattle often fared badly. The settlers, in order to prevent their cattle from starving, were forced to cut down trees so that they could browse on the buds and young branches. The women were required to clear land and do rough farmwork, such as harrowing, harvesting, hoeing corn, etc. They were also accustomed to other phases of hard pioneer life.

Large quantities of maple sugar and molasses were in a few years manufactured by the settlers of the Conemaugh country and packed to neighboring settlements. Venison also became an article of traffic. In exchange for these commodities the Conemaugh settlers received the necessaries which they could not produce themselves. Bedford was their principal market.

In the course of time the population of Conemaugh-town increased as well as the number of farms in its vicinity. A log inn for the entertainment of travelers was built. A road was opened through the wilderness to Frankstown, below Hollidaysburg, upon which bar iron was hauled to Conemaugh-town and shipped in the spring of the year in flat-bottomed boats to Pittsburgh. Conemaugh-town now became a place of some business, and it was found necessary to build another inn.

In 1808 the town was overflowed by a sudden rise in the Conemaugh and Stony creek and the inhabitants were compelled to fly to the hills for safety. The town was again submerged in 1816. This event was termed "the punkin flood," owing to the fact that it swept away the whole pumpkin crop of that year. Much damage was done by this flood. Fences were swept away, saw-logs and lumber disappeared, and many horses and cattle were drowned. The settlers suffered severely by this flood.

About 1812 the town boasted a grist mill and also a small iron forge on Stony creek. In 1816 the first keel boat was built by Isaac Proctor on the right bank of the Stony creek, near where the Union graveyard is located. Flatboats were also constructed at the same place. While laborers were digging the race for another forge on the Conemaugh old fire-brands, pieces of blankets, an earthen smoke-pipe, and other Indian relics were discovered at a depth of twelve feet below the surface of the earth.

Notwithstanding the improvements mentioned the town was still small when, about 1829, the Commonwealth commenced the construction of the Canal and Portage Railroad. Since that time it has steadily prospered and gradually become a place of some note and business importance.

REVELATIONS OF AN OLD LEDGER.

FROM THE BULLETIN OF THE AMERICAN IRON AND STEEL ASSOCIATION FOR JUNE 1, 1896.

JOHNSTOWN has had three periods of transportation development—the first embracing the flatboat era from about 1800 to 1830; the second beginning with the completion of the Pennsylvania Canal to Johnstown in 1830 and extending to the completion of the Pennsylvania Railroad to Pittsburgh in 1852; and the third beginning with the completion of the Pennsylvania Railroad and extending to the present time. The iron industry of Johnstown has also had three periods of development—the first embracing Cambria forge at Johnstown and Shade furnace, Shade forge, and Mary Ann forge in Somerset county near Johnstown, all of which were built between 1808 and 1820; the second, a ten-year period, embracing Cambria, Ben's Creek, Mill Creek, Mount Vernon, and Somerset furnaces, built from 1842 to 1846—Mount Vernon in Johnstown and the other furnaces only a few miles away; and the third beginning with the organization of the Cambria Iron Company in 1852 and coming down to the present time.

Johnstown owes its start as an industrial and commercial centre to the fact that its location at the head of flatboat navigation on the Conemaugh furnished an outlet for the iron of the Juniata valley at the beginning of the nineteenth century. There was more water in the Conemaugh and its tributaries in those years than there is now. Johnstown was an iron town before Pittsburgh had made a pound of iron. The following details deal exclusively with the period of flatboat transportation and with the first period of the iron industry of Johnstown.

For the facts that we shall present we are in part indebted to an old ledger which has recently come into our possession and which escaped the destruction of the Johnstown flood in 1889. The ledger contains accounts of sales made and of credits entered by Isaac Proctor, a merchant of Johnstown in the early years of the nineteenth century, and a record of other business transactions by Mr. Proctor. His store was located on Main street, immediately opposite the site of the First Presbyterian church.

Isaac Proctor was a native of Bedford county, Pennsylvania. He settled at Johnstown, " at the forks of the Conemaugh," when it was a mere hamlet of log houses, soon after 1800, in which year the town was "laid out" by Joseph Johns, a Swiss Mennonite, into streets and alleys, building lots, public squares, and other reservations. But the name that was then officially given to the new town was Conemaugh and not Johnstown, the latter name being substituted for the former in 1834. We have before us a letter dated at Conemaugh on April 27, 1832. Settlements had been made at Johnstown before 1800 by German and Swiss farmers. For a number of years after 1800 the town was almost entirely inhabited by people of German and Swiss origin.

Isaac Proctor was not only a country merchant but he was also the owner of a warehouse on the north bank of Stony creek, below Franklin street, in Johnstown, which was maintained for the express purpose of receiving and storing bar iron from the forges of the Juniata valley, which bar iron was hauled to Johnstown over the Frankstown Road and thence shipped in flatboats to Pittsburgh by way of the Conemaugh, Kiskiminitas, and Allegheny rivers. There were other warehouses near that of Isaac Proctor which were maintained for precisely the same purpose. The flatboats were built at Johnstown or at points farther up the Stony creek and as far south as the mouth of Ben's creek, three miles away. A large business was done far into the nineteenth century in the shipment of Juniata iron by flatboats from Johnstown. At first and for many years these shipments embraced only bar iron, but subsequently and down to the opening of the Pennsylvania Canal to Johnstown late in 1830 they embraced also blooms and pig iron, all made with charcoal. As the navigation of the streams mentioned was as yet wholly unimproved shipments could only be made during high water, and even then experienced pilots were needed to prevent the boats from going to pieces on the rocks and riffles in which the Conemaugh river particularly abounded. Occasionally a boat was wrecked. In one disaster at Richards' Falls two lives were lost. Much of the hauling over the Frankstown Road was done on sleds in the winter, and February and March, when the spring break-up took place, were favorite months for sending the flatboats to Pittsburgh, one hundred miles away. The boats were sold at Pittsburgh and the crews walked home.

Keel boats were also used on the Conemaugh and Kiskiminitas rivers, but they were used chiefly in the salt trade, the Conemaugh salt works beginning about forty miles west of Johnstown. The first salt works on the Conemaugh date from about 1814. In A. J. Hite's *Hand Book of Johnstown*, printed in 1856, it is stated that the first keel boat built at Johnstown was built by Isaac Proctor in 1816. Keel boats, which passed from the Conemaugh and Kiskiminitas into the Allegheny, brought return cargoes from Pittsburgh.

The merchandise accounts in Mr. Proctor's ledger are chiefly for the years 1808 and 1809, occasional entries coming down as late as 1810, 1811, and 1812. The warehouse accounts are for the years 1816, 1817, and 1818. As is usual in ledger accounts the prices of merchandise are not often given. It is, however, very remarkable that all the merchandise accounts are kept in pounds, shillings, and pence. The pound character (£) is used. Dollars and cents are nowhere mentioned, although our Federal coinage was authorized in 1792 and silver dollars were coined as early as 1794. The dollar mark ($) does not appear in any of the merchandise accounts. That business should have been transacted in British or colonial currency in an interior town in Pennsylvania as late as 1812 is a discovery for which we were not prepared. We can not understand why the British system of computing values was continued in that interior town so long, nor is any light thrown upon the value of a pound in dollars and cents at Johnstown in 1812, or upon the forms of currency that were used when payments were made in "cash." John Holliday closed his account

with Mr. Proctor in June, 1811, when he is credited with
a payment of £32 16s. 4d. in "cash;" in January, 1811,
Patrick Dempsey closed his account by giving his note for
£6 10s. 3d.; in 1812 William Fulford closed his account
by giving his note for £2 6s. 1d.; and in the same year
John Grosenickle closed his account by giving his note for
£1 1s. 2d. In 1808 John Grosenickle is credited with £1
11s. 9d. for hauling a load of maple sugar to Bedford.
There are other entries in the same denominations.

Another revelation of this old ledger is just as remarkable as the use of pounds, shillings, and pence until 1812.
The warehouse accounts of bar iron received and shipped
in 1816, 1817, and 1818 are kept in tons, hundredweights,
quarters, and pounds, the ton representing 2,240 pounds,
the hundredweight 112 pounds, and the quarter 28 pounds.
The teamsters who hauled bar iron over the Frankstown
Road are credited in tons, hundredweights, quarters, and
pounds, and shipments to Pittsburgh are entered in the
same terms. In ordinary commercial transactions neither
iron nor any other commodity has been weighed by hundredweights and quarters forming fractions of a gross ton
at any time within our recollection, the usage being to
weigh only by tons and pounds, and it is really very surprising that the English custom should have prevailed at
Johnstown at so late a day as we have mentioned. Charges for storage in 1816, 1817, and 1818 appear, however, to
have been paid in dollars and cents, as we find several
charges in 1818 in these denominations. We have also
found within the leaves of the ledger a bill against Isaac
Proctor which reads as follows : "Juniata Forge, 16th December, 1818. Mr. Isaac Proctor Bot of Peter Shoenberger
2 qrs. 1 lb. Bar Iron, @ $0.08c—$4.56." Juniata forge was
located at Petersburg, in Huntingdon county, and it was
built about 1804. In 1814 or 1815 it passed into the hands
of Dr. Peter Shoenberger.

The numerous entries in Mr. Proctor's ledger make clear
the fact that large quantities of bar iron were shipped at
Johnstown by flatboats in 1816, 1817, and 1818. He did a
large warehousing business and other owners of warehouses
were probably active competitors. The aggregate tonnage

shipped by Mr. Proctor, which was chiefly on account of Dr. Shoenberger, amounted to several hundred tons annually. Some of Mr. Proctor's shipments amounted to 16 and 19 tons. Some of these shipments were made " in my own boat," which was doubtless a keel boat. Pittsburgh antiquarians may be interested in learning that the consignees of bar iron at Pittsburgh in those days were Richard Bowen & Co., Robert Alexander, Allen & Grant, Charles McGee, J. Whiting, Robinson, McNickel & Wilds, Irwin & George, and Thomas Jackson.

The chief interest of this old ledger consists in its revelation of the fact that large quantities of Juniata bar iron were shipped to Pittsburgh from Johnstown as early as 1816. Earlier shipments were made by water from Johnstown to the same destination, probably as early as 1800, but the ledger of Isaac Proctor shows conclusively that these shipments had attained large proportions in 1816, 1817, and 1818, in which years bar iron had not yet been made at Pittsburgh. Next in importance among the facts disclosed by Mr. Proctor's ledger is the survival at Johnstown down to 1812 of the British system of computing values, and the survival down to 1818 of the now long disused hundredweights and quarters.

From other sources than the old ledger we add some other facts which show the prominence of Johnstown as an iron centre early in the nineteenth century.

John Holliday built a forge at Johnstown, on the right bank of the Stony creek, about 1809, for the manufacture of bar iron from Juniata blooms and pig iron, but we find no mention in Mr. Proctor's ledger of any shipments from this forge. The dam of this forge was washed away about 1811, and subsequently the forge was removed to the north bank of the Conemaugh, in the Millville addition to Johnstown, where it was operated down to about 1822, Rahm & Bean, of Pittsburgh, being the lessees at this time. In 1817 Thomas Burrell, the proprietor at that time, offered woodcutters " fifty cents per cord for chopping two thousand cords of wood at Cambria forge, Johnstown." The forge would appear to have been in operation from 1809 to 1822.

In 1807 or 1808 Shade furnace was built on Shade

creek, in Somerset county, about fifteen miles southeast of Johnstown, and in 1820 Shade forge was built near the furnace. As early as 1820 bar iron was shipped to Pittsburgh from Shade forge. Much of the iron from this forge was hauled to Johnstown and thence shipped to Pittsburgh, but some of it was shipped in flatboats directly from the forge. Pig iron was also hauled to Johnstown from Shade furnace for shipment to Pittsburgh. But there was another early forge, which was still nearer to Johnstown, on the Stony creek, about half a mile below the mouth of Shade creek, known as Mary Ann forge, which shipped bar iron to Pittsburgh at a still earlier day, and perhaps as early as 1811. Richard Geary, the father of Governor John W. Geary, was the manager of the forge for about one year, and was supercargo of a load of bar iron which was shipped from the forge down the Stony creek, the Conemaugh, and other streams to Pittsburgh. Garret Ream lived at the mouth of Ben's creek and built boats which were loaded at Johnstown, but he also shipped iron direct from Ben's creek, and it is probable that some of this iron came from Mary Ann forge, Shade furnace, and Shade forge.

About 200 pounds of nails, valued at $30, were made at Johnstown by one establishment in the census year 1810. About this time an enterprise was established at Johnstown by Robert Pierson, by whom nails were cut from strips of so-called "nail iron" with a machine worked by a treadle, but without heads, which were added by hand in a vise. The "nail iron" was obtained at the small rolling mills in Huntingdon county and hauled in wagons or sleds to Johnstown over the Frankstown Road.

REV. SHADRACH HOWELL TERRY.

FIRST PASTOR OF THE FIRST PRESBYTERIAN CHURCH OF JOHNSTOWN. WRITTEN IN 1898.*

I HAVE been requested to prepare a sketch of the life of Rev. S. H. Terry, the first pastor of the First Presbyterian church of Johnstown. Unaided I could not comply with this request, but with the assistance of Hon. Cyrus L. Pershing, Rev. Dr. B. L. Agnew, and others I present the following summary of all the facts that are accessible concerning the life of this early Johnstown preacher of the Gospel, whose remains now rest in Grand View cemetery, which overlooks the scene of his last and most successful labors. It is a beautiful spot for a city of the dead.

"Around this lovely valley rise
The purple hills of Paradise."

The full name of Mr. Terry was Shadrach Howell Terry. He always wrote it S. H. Terry in a cramped, nervous hand. Mr. Terry was born on Long Island in 1795. He graduated at Yale College in 1819, under that prince of educators in his time, Jeremiah Day. His theological training was received at Princeton. This information I have received from Judge Pershing, who also advises me that Mr. Terry's father was for a time a member of the New York Legislature. Judge Pershing also says that Mr. Terry showed to him more than once a volume which had been presented to him by Dr. Day, the president of Yale College, for excelling in oratory. It will be seen that Mr. Terry's educational advantages were excellent and fully in keeping with the traditions of the Presbyterian Church. He probably entered the Presbyterian ministry soon after 1820, and

---

* This sketch, which I prepared by request, was read by the pastor, Rev. C. C. Hays, D.D., to a large congregation gathered in the First Presbyterian church of Johnstown on Sunday evening, March 6, 1898. I have added some information about other early Johnstown churches.

as his wife was a native of Delaware he probably preached for a time in that State before coming to Pennsylvania. It is not known at what time he came to Pennsylvania, but it is certain that he was in 1830 the pastor of the Presbyterian congregations of Somerset and Jenner, in Somerset county, within the bounds of the Presbytery of Redstone. Mrs. Mary A. Parks, of the fifth ward of Johnstown, remembers very well when Mr. Terry resided and preached in Somerset. He did not reside at Somerset longer than a year or two, removing from there to Jenner, now Jennerstown, which was then a place of more promise than it is now, and at which place he continued to reside until his removal to Johnstown, in the meantime serving the congregations of both Jenner and Somerset.

We must now go back a few years. About 1820 the Protestant citizens of Johnstown, which then embraced a population of only a few hundred persons, united in building a one-story frame house on a lot of ground near the foot of Market street, which was donated for school purposes by Joseph Johns in 1800, and which lot has come to be known as the Union school lot and the building and its successors as the Union school-house. In this building the children of the first settlers of Johnstown were taught in subscription schools the rudiments of an English education, the common-school system not then having been established in Pennsylvania, and in this building were also held religious services, the few Protestants of the town using it alternately or together. This arrangement did not always give satisfaction, and as early as 1829, as I learn from Mr. Wesley J. Rose, the Methodists fitted up a warehouse that had been used for the storage of iron, and which stood where the United Brethren church now stands on Vine street, and worshiped in it until 1838, when they occupied their new church on the site of the present Methodist church at the corner of Franklin and Locust streets. The warehouse and the lot of ground on which it stood were donated by Peter Levergood, himself a Lutheran.

In his " History of the Churches in Blairsville Presbytery " Rev. Dr. Alexander Donaldson says that " Johnstown, where an independent church had a brief previous existence,

was first supplied with Presbyterian preaching on October
31, 1830, by Rev. Shadrach Howell Terry, of Redstone Presbytery." This sermon was preached in the Union school-
house.* The Presbytery of Blairsville was formed in 1830
from the Presbytery of Redstone and held its first meeting
on November 16 of that year. It will be remembered that
it was in this year that Mr. Terry was engaged as pastor
at Somerset. When Dr. Donaldson referred to " an independent church " at Johnstown he had in mind, as I learn
from Dr. Agnew, the Congregational, or Independent, church
which had been organized by Rev. George Roberts, of
Ebensburg, with five members, all women. This was the
first organized church in Johnstown. It existed until 1825,
when the pastor, Mr. Timothy C. Davies, was dismissed and
soon afterwards the organization disbanded. Mrs. Jane Mc-
Kee was a member of this church and was also one of
the fifteen original members of the Presbyterian church of
Johnstown which was subsequently organized.

Until 1836 Mr. Davies was a clerk in the office of John
Matthews, the first collector of tolls on the Pennsylvania
Canal at Johnstown. He subsequently taught school at
Johnstown and established a brewery on Main street, below
Market street. About 1840 he moved away from Johnstown.

Dr. Donaldson says that, by consent of the Presbyteries
of Redstone and Blairsville, Mr. Terry began on August 1,
1832, to supply the church at Johnstown one-fourth of his
time, and that, "on December 14, 1832, Rev. Samuel Swan
organized a Presbyterian church at Johnstown, consisting of
fifteen members, with Shepley Priestley, James Brown, and
William Graham as elders." Judge Pershing says that Mr.
Terry preached in the Union school-house, and that his
father, who was a great admirer of Mr. Terry, often took
him when a small boy to the school-house to hear Mr. Terry
preach. Dr. Agnew says that Mr. Terry's compensation for

---

* In Joseph Johns' charter of the town of Conemaugh, now Johnstown, dated at Somerset, November 3, 1800, he made the following provision : " The said Joseph Johns hereby gives and grants to the said
future inhabitants two certain lots of ground situate on Market street
and Chestnut street, in the said town, marked in the general plan
thereof No. 133 and No. 134, for the purpose of erecting school-houses and
houses of public worship, free and clear of all incumbrances whatsoever."

one-fourth of his time at Johnstown was $100 a year. He
was at this time a resident of Jenner, twenty miles away,
and served the congregation at Somerset as well as the congregations at Jenner and Johnstown. Irrespective of the
small salary paid that was a hard life to lead, especially
when the roads and the weather were bad. Dr. Donaldson's
account of Mr. Terry's further connection with the church
at Johnstown is substantially as follows:

"In 1835 Mr. Terry became a member of Blairsville Presbytery, and having accepted a call for half time as pastor
of the Johnstown church he was installed on November 13,
1835. Rev. D. Lewis preached, Rev. T. Davis charged the
pastor, and Rev. Samuel Swan the people. The other half
of his time was given to Armagh. During the summer of
1835 a commodious brick house of worship was erected at
Johnstown and was dedicated on Christmas day, the beginning of a communion season. Mr. Terry's health failing
he gradually diminished his labors at Armagh until October 6, 1840, when Johnstown secured all his time. This
church being noticed to be in the territory of Huntingdon Presbytery and Synod of Philadelphia the Presbytery
of Blairsville requested the General Assembly of 1839 to
change the line of synods so as to place Cambria county
in the Synod of Pittsburgh and the Presbytery of Blairsville, which was done.

"On the night of Wednesday, May 26, 1841, Mr. Terry
was attacked with bilious pleurisy, which terminated his life
and labors on June 3d, in the 46th year of his age. Rev.
Samuel Swan, being there to assist at a communion, preached
a funeral sermon from Rev. 14: 13. The salary was continued for six months and a sandstone monument erected
over his remains by the congregation. It is now much defaced by time. The communion on that occasion was ad-
ministered by Mr. Swan, and for him a call was moderated
by Rev. David Kirkpatrick on August 16th, accepted on
October 5th, and his installation as pastor occurred on November 9th of the same year."

In what I have quoted from Dr. Donaldson I have made
some corrections upon the superior authority of Dr. Agnew.
Mr. Terry was buried in the Union graveyard, adjoining

the ground donated by Mr. Johns on which the Union school-house was built. The ground for the graveyard had also been donated by Mr. Johns.

After coming to Johnstown Mr. Swan also served the congregation at Armagh, beginning in 1845, as Mr. Terry had previously done. The trips to Armagh were usually made on horseback by both pastors on the towpath of the Pennsylvania Canal. Like Jenner the present hamlet of Armagh was at one time a place of some promise. Mr. Swan had previously, beginning in 1824, been the pastor of several congregations in Ligonier valley. From 1841 to 1845 Mr. Swan's salary at Johnstown was $500 a year.

In December, 1869, Rev. William A. Fleming, then the pastor of the Presbyterian church of Johnstown, wrote to Rev. Dr. B. L. Agnew, at Philadelphia, for such information as he possessed concerning Mr. Terry and received a letter from the doctor, under date of December 20, 1869, which now lies before me and ·from which I glean the following additional facts. The congregational meeting at which Mr. Terry was called to give half his time to the church at Johnstown was held in the warehouse of Dr. Agnew's father, Mr. Smith Agnew, on May 4, 1835, and about the same time Mr. Terry received a call from the Armagh congregation for the other half. The Johnstown call was moderated by the Rev. Samuel McFarren and the Armagh call was moderated by the Rev. Samuel Swan. The Johnstown congregation agreed to pay Mr. Terry a salary of $250 a year and the Armagh congregation agreed to pay $150, making $400 in all. Dr. Agnew says that the Presbytery of Redstone promptly dissolved the pastoral relation existing between Mr. Terry and the congregations of Somerset and Jenner and dismissed him to the Presbytery of Blairsville. When Mr. Terry in 1840 gave his whole time to the Johnstown congregation his salary was fixed at $400 a year. Dr. Agnew also says that Mr. Terry's ministry at Johnstown from the time of his first call in 1832 to his death in 1841 was remarkably successful, 131 additions to the communion of the church having been added in that period. From 1830, when Mr. Terry preached his first sermon in Johnstown, until his death in 1841 was almost eleven years.

From 1835 to 1898 the First Presbyterian church of Johnstown has had eight regular pastors, whose names I mention in the order of their service: Rev. S. H. Terry, Rev. Samuel Swan, Rev. Ross Stevenson, Rev. Dr. Benjamin L. Agnew, Rev. William A. Fleming, Rev. D. M. Miller, Rev. D. J. Beale, and Rev. C. C. Hays.

It has already been stated that, in the summer of 1835, in which year Mr. Terry agreed to give half his time to the Johnstown church and the other half to the church at Armagh, "a commodious brick house of worship" was erected at Johnstown. This church building stood exactly on the site of the present First Presbyterian church of Johnstown. That the Johnstown congregation was at this time sufficiently strong in numbers to erect a substantial house of worship was due largely to the successful ministrations of Mr. Terry during the period from 1832 to 1835, in which he preached one-fourth of his time at Johnstown. Dr. Agnew says that the lot of ground on which the church edifice was built was sold to the congregation by John Barnes, who was a wagon-maker, a native of England, for $200. One-half of this sum was paid on August 14, 1834, and the other half was paid in September, 1842, when the deed was executed. This lot is now one of the most valuable lots in Johnstown. Mr. Rose says that the Fuller brothers were the stone masons of the new church, that Joseph Haynes was the brickmaker and bricklayer, and that Emanuel Shaffer was the carpenter.

During the pastorate of Dr. Agnew the church edifice of 1835 was torn down and the present edifice was erected. The last sermon in the old church was preached by Dr. Agnew on Sunday, August 23, 1863. During the erection of the present building the congregation worshiped in the town hall for a time and then in the Methodist Protestant church on Franklin street. The basement of the new church was opened for service on Sunday, September 3, 1865, and the whole building was dedicated in April, 1866.

Quoting from Dr. Donaldson I have already mentioned that the first ruling elders of the Presbyterian church of Johnstown, elected in 1832, were Shepley Priestley, James Brown, and William Graham. Dr. Donaldson adds that on

July 26, 1835, Smith Agnew, Samuel Douglass, (tanner,) and Samuel Kennedy were ordained as elders, probably to succeed Messrs. Priestley, Brown, and Graham, and that on April 26, 1839, Henry Kratzer and Moses Canan were also ordained as elders, probably to succeed Messrs. Agnew and Douglass, who had left Johnstown.

Dr. Agnew furnishes me with the following list of the original members of the Presbyterian church of Johnstown in 1832, when the church was organized, Mr. Terry giving to it one-fourth of his time, as has already been stated: Mr. and Mrs. Shepley Priestley, William Graham and his wife, Mrs. Esther Graham, Mr. and Mrs. Samuel Douglass, Mrs. Jane McKee, Mrs. Ann Linton, Mrs. Caroline White, Mr. John McClane and his wife, Mrs. Julia McClane, Mrs. Nancy Hayes, Mrs. Elizabeth Eckels, Mrs. Jane Kooken, and Mr. James Brown. Many persons then attended the services of the church and contributed to its support who were not members of its communion. As late as 1869 three of the original members of 1832 were still living. All are now dead. Our honored fellow-citizen, John White, now in his 91st year, was one of Mr. Terry's earliest communicants. Mr. White has seen General Arthur St. Clair, a soldier of the Revolution. This was in 1818.

In the spring of 1834 Smith Agnew came to Johnstown with his family from Warren, Armstrong county, now Apollo, where Dr. Agnew was born in 1833, and built a warehouse on the south side of the canal basin in the same year. In 1837 Mr. Agnew removed from Johnstown to New Alexandria, Westmoreland county, and a few years afterwards he again changed his residence to Greensburg. It has already been stated that the congregational meeting at which a call was extended to Mr. Terry for one-half his time was held in Mr. Agnew's warehouse in 1835.

Dr. Agnew says that a Union Sunday-school had been organized at an early day in the Union school-house, under the auspices of the Congregationalists, or Independents, already mentioned, but in 1834 the Lutherans and Methodists withdrew from this school. On January 18, 1835, while still worshiping in the Union school-house, a Presbyterian Sunday-school was organized in the same building and

Smith Agnew was elected its first superintendent. He continued to act as its superintendent until his removal from Johnstown two years later.

Dr. Agnew furnishes me with the following list of the teachers in the Presbyterian Sunday-school at its organization in January, 1835 : Samuel Kennedy, Henry Kratzer, Evan Roberts, Charles B. Ellis, Emanuel Shaffer, John Barnes, David R. Lamb, Sarah Priestley, Margaret McKee, Elizabeth McKee, Elizabeth Priestley, Elizabeth Graham, Elizabeth McCreary, Elizabeth Barnes, Pamilla Livermore, and Martha Moore.

Mr. Terry removed his family from Jenner to Johnstown late in 1835. It consisted of himself, his wife, and two children—a son, John Henry, and a daughter, Mary Elizabeth. Mrs. Terry's maiden name was Elizabeth Ponder and her home was at Milton, Delaware. She was of Quaker birth and education and she appears to have never entirely surrendered her Quaker convictions. Her family was once prominent in Delaware. Judge Pershing, from whom I obtain these facts, says that one of her relatives named James Ponder was once Governor of Delaware.

Judge Pershing's recollection is that Mr. Terry lived in 1836 in a little house on the east side of Jackson street, just north of Main street. In 1837 or 1838 he moved to the McClure house, on Canal street, now Washington street, above the McConaughy tanyard and on the south side of the street. In 1839 he occupied the Lutheran parsonage, on the right bank of the Stony creek. In 1840 he lived in Thomas Quinn's brick house, on the east side of Franklin street, on the corner of the alley nearest to Canal street. In 1841 he moved to the brick house on the south side of Main street, on the corner of the alley above Dibert's store. Here he died. This house was the first brick house built in Johnstown, if we except a small brick house built by Joseph Haynes at his brickyard on the south side of the Stony creek. The house on Main street, which is still standing, was built in 1828 by Adam Bausman with brick made and laid by Joseph Haynes.

While living in the McClure house in the winter of 1838 Mr. Terry taught a subscription school for one term of probably three months in a small building which stood on the bank of the canal almost opposite his residence. This building was afterwards purchased by James Purse, who built an addition to it and lived in it until he died. Among Mr. Terry's pupils Judge Pershing remembers the following: Catherine Swegler, Elizabeth Purse, Catherine Jane Roberts, Sarah J. Royer, Mary L. Royer, Matilda Sheridan, Charlotte L. Canan, S. Dean Canan, A. Frank Royer, R. H. Patterson, Charles Davis, Ann Davis, Cyrus L. Pershing, and John Henry Terry. By permission of Collector Potts Mr. Terry occupied the office of the collector one winter, probably the winter of 1839, as a recitation room for a small class of boys who studied Latin and mathematics, perhaps also a little Greek, under his direction. This class was composed of R. H. Patterson, afterwards Dr. Patterson, of Stoyestown, Somerset county, who boarded with Mr. Terry; Richard Peters, of Blairsville; and Cyrus L. Pershing, Israel C. Pershing, Campbell Sheridan, Charles M. Priestley, and John Henry Terry, of Johnstown. Cyrus L. Pershing, and possibly others, recited Latin to Mr. Terry privately to the day of his last illness. It may be mentioned also that Cyrus L. Pershing and Campbell Sheridan recited Greek to Rev. Mr. Swan in 1842 to prepare themselves to enter the freshman class of Jefferson College.

Judge Pershing tells me that he and Campbell Sheridan, now Dr. Sheridan, sat up with Mr. Terry the last night he lived.* They left him about daylight, Sheridan to go to the office of James Potts, the collector of tolls on the Pennsylvania Canal, where he was a clerk, and Pershing to go to the office of Thomas Lever, at the canal weighlock, where he also was a clerk. About 9 o'clock both of these

*Judge Pershing kept a diary in 1841, and from this diary the Judge sends me the following extracts: "May 26, 1841—Wednesday.—I recited my last lesson to Mr. Terry in the weighlock office, from Virgil. . . . Mr. Terry spent the day at Mr. Coshun's, and after his return home in the evening was attacked suddenly with bilious pleurisy. . . . June 2. —Campbell Sheridan and I remained all night with Mr. Terry. He was 'flighty' the greater part of the night, and evidently sinking very fast. . . . June 3—Thursday.—Mr. Terry died this morning a little after 9 o'clock. He was buried June 4. His funeral sermon was preached by Rev. Samuel Swan."

young men, who afterwards became ruling elders in the church founded by Mr. Terry and successively superintendents of its Sunday-school, were shocked to hear of his death. I can myself remember very well how greatly the whole town was shocked and grieved to learn that Mr. Terry had passed away. I was a pupil at Robert H. Canan's subscription school at the time, and when Mr. Canan heard the sad news he promptly dismissed his school out of respect to Mr. Terry's memory. Mr. Terry died on Thursday morning, June 3. His last words were these: "I have preached Christ to this people." These dying words would form an appropriate inscription on the new monument which it is proposed to erect over Mr. Terry's grave in Grand View cemetery. (This has been done.)

An obituary notice of Mr. Terry was prepared soon after his death by Moses Canan, one of Mr. Terry's elders, and published in *The Presbyterian,* of Philadelphia. I have seen this notice in the files of *The Presbyterian.* It is very brief but is valuable as an estimate of Mr. Terry's character as a man and a minister.

Mr. Terry died intestate, as the lawyers say, that is he did not leave a will, and it became necessary that the court should appoint an administrator of his estate, which, it may be easily surmised, was very small. Samuel Kennedy was appointed administrator. Robert L. Johnston was the auditor appointed by the court to adjust the account of Mr. Kennedy. Judge Pershing tells me that Mr. Terry was often in straitened circumstances while he lived in Johnstown. He was always paid a meagre salary.

Mr. Terry was a small man, about five feet seven inches high, and weighed about 135 pounds. He was neat in his dress and reserved and dignified in his general intercourse with men. A small dining table, which was owned by Mr. Terry at his death, is now a precious possession of the Johnstown congregation.

As has already been mentioned, Mr. Terry's remains were laid to rest in the Union graveyard and a plain sandstone monument was erected by the congregation. The monument, including the base, was scarcely five feet high. Dr. Donaldson says that the monument was much defaced

by time in 1874, when his history of the Blairsville Presbytery was published. The monument, if it ever deserved
the name, had, however, been defaced for many years before
1874, and it continued to be defaced and the grave marked
by it to be neglected for many years after that year. In
1888, the year before the Johnstown flood, three public-
spirited citizens of Johnstown, not all of them members of
the church founded by Mr. Terry or of any church communion, purchased a lot in Grand View cemetery and removed
to it the remains of Mr. Terry and also the long defaced
monument. The removal took place in the fall of 1888.
If the intention of these citizens to remove the remains
of Mr. Terry had not been carried into effect in 1888 the
removal could never have been made, as the flood of the
following May would have dashed to pieces the monument
and forever have obliterated all vestige of the grave itself.

Soon after Mr. Terry's death his wife and children removed to Philadelphia, where a brother of Mrs. Terry was
then living. It was a most unfortunate change. Mrs. Terry
was poor and probably often in want the remainder of her
days. Mr. Terry had built up the Presbyterian congregation at Johnstown through many years of self-denying service and the congregation should have cared for his widow
and fatherless children better than it did.

Judge Pershing says that, of the two children left by Mr.
Terry, the son, John Henry, became a sailor. On a voyage
between Philadelphia and Charleston he fell from the rig-
ging of the vessel and was injured so badly that he died
shortly afterwards in a hospital at Charleston. The other
child, Mary Elizabeth, was married in Philadelphia to an
oysterman named Glazer. Dr. Agnew says that Mrs. Terry
died in Philadelphia on November 30, 1867, at the home of
her daughter, and that her son, John Henry, died on August
8, 1868, as the result of the fall mentioned by Judge Pershing, which Dr. Agnew says occurred during a storm off
Cape Hatteras. Mrs. Glazer, who is described by Judge
Pershing as "a pretty, bright little girl" when she lived in
Johnstown, was living in extremely humble circumstances
in Philadelphia when Dr. Agnew called upon her in 1868
or 1869. Since then all traces of her have been lost.

RECOLLECTIONS OF EARLY JOHNSTOWN.

WRITTEN IN 1909 TO REV. C. C. HAYS, D. D., PASTOR OF THE
FIRST PRESBYTERIAN CHURCH OF JOHNSTOWN.

DEAR DOCTOR : In compliance with your request I write
you briefly concerning the Presbyterian Sunday-school of
seventy years ago in Johnstown as I remember it. Rev.
Shadrach Howell Terry was then the pastor of the congregation, but he died in 1841, when he was succeeded by
Rev. Samuel Swan. It was in 1839 that my father and
mother first sent me to the Sunday-school (we did not call
it Sabbath-school) which met then and for many years
afterwards in the Presbyterian church of that day, occupying the site of the present structure. The building, which
was of brick, contained only one large room, with no other
furniture whatever than a pulpit, pews, four cannon stoves
with their long pipes, and strips of carpet in the aisles. I
do not think that there was a cushioned pew in the whole
church. There was no musical instrument except Judge
Roberts's tuning fork, which he used as the leader of the
unpaid choir, the congregation always joining in the sing-
ing. The church was entered by two front doors, which
communicated with two main aisles, and the choir occupied
pews just inside the doors and facing the pulpit. The
church was first lighted at night with tallow candles, held
in position by tin sconces hung on nails between the windows, but lard-oil and sperm-oil lamps were used in the
pulpit. Subsequently lamps of the same character were
used throughout the building, and these in time were dis-
placed by camphene lamps, after which came petroleum
lamps. The church was not hemmed in by other buildings
in too close proximity but " stood four-square to all the
winds that blew." It was therefore in daytime well lighted.
    It was in the room, or auditorium, which I have briefly
described that the Presbyterian Sunday-school assembled

every Sunday at 9 o'clock in summer and at 2 o'clock in winter. Boys and girls of all ages attended and were classified chiefly according to their common school attainments, with some regard also, of course, to their ages. There was no high-sounding " Bible class," but several classes studied the Bible regularly with the help of a series of Union Question Books, which were well printed and bound in blue covers. I remember particularly that one volume was devoted to Exodus and another to the Acts of the Apostles. Our teachers led us from point to point and from place to place, with comments that were interesting and instructive. No question was ever raised in these classes about the inspiration of every word of the Bible; that was taken for granted. We all grew up in those days with reverence for the Holy Book and with considerable knowledge of its contents. Other classes recited the Shorter Catechism and read biblical selections. The classes composed of little boys and little girls were taught very much as they are now. Each class occupied a pew and each teacher occupied a pew in front of his or her class. We had a superintendent and a librarian.

Now about our teachers. I am writing of a period which extended from 1839 to 1850. Moses Canan, a lawyer of Scotch-Irish origin, a ruling elder in the church and often superintendent of the school, was the oldest of the teachers in years. He was one of the most impressive readers I have ever heard. George W. Munson and S. H. Smith, prominent business men of New England extraction, were good teachers. So also were James Potts and Henry Kratzer, the former born of Scotch-Irish parents and the latter a Pennsylvania German. So also were Campbell Sheridan and Cyrus L. Pershing, young men of liberal education, who afterwards became superintendents of the Sunday-school, ruling elders in the church, and prominent in the professions of their choice. Both were natives of Western Pennsylvania. There were other teachers, including many ladies, whom I need not mention, if indeed I could remember the names of all of them. There was always a full attendance of " scholars," and I think that there was never a scarcity of teachers. All the teachers I have mentioned by name were at one time or another in charge of classes which used the Union Question Books above referred to.

Connected with the school was a carefully selected library of well-printed books, from which every "scholar" could select one volume every Sunday, returning it the next Sunday. There was also a monthly missionary paper, well printed and freely illustrated, a copy of which was given to each of us as often as it appeared. How proud we were of these literary treasures—the handsomely-bound books especially! The books, of which there was a goodly number, covered almost every subject that would interest a healthy boy or girl; not one of them was of a sectarian character. We had books that inspired and ministered to a love of the history of our own and of other countries; books devoted to natural history; books about the North American Indians, the natives of Iceland, the Sandwich Islands, and the "heathen" everywhere; books that described the manners, customs, and habits of the civilized or half-civilized people of other countries than our own. We had Peter Parley's books, the Rollo books, and a series entitled "Travels About Home." I think that there was not a work of fiction in the whole library, although there could not have been any possible objection to such story books as "Robinson Crusoe" and the "Swiss Family Robinson." Perhaps we did have them; I hope so. Any way the boys of our school all read these stories and talked about them, and, of course, the girls did too. We had Bunyan's "Pilgrim's Progress," "Sanford and Merton," and "The Shepherd of Salisbury Plain." The tendency of all the books in the library was to stimulate a love of good books, and without a love of such books no boy or girl will ever amount to very much. That we could get a new book every Sunday was one of the strongest reasons why we were glad to attend the Sunday-school at all.

Now I am told that the library of sixty and seventy years ago no longer exists—that the boys and girls who attend the Presbyterian Sunday-school no longer carry home with them books of the character of those I have described. Instead I am informed that these boys and girls are compelled to rely mainly on the Cambria Library for reading matter, and that the books they obtain at the library are largely modern works of fiction. What books, if any, little children can get at the Cambria Library that will take the place of the books that are printed especially for Sunday-school children I am not informed. Is the substitution of modern works of fiction for the well-selected books of the Presbyterian Sunday-school of long ago a change for the better or the worse? Undoubtedly it is for the worse. No thoughtful person will say otherwise.

William F. Prosser, the son of David Prosser and about one year my junior, was one of the Presbyterian Sunday-school "scholars" in 1840, 1841, and 1842, and the only one except myself that I feel sure is now living. Growing to manhood elsewhere he made an honorable record in the civil war, at its close being colonel of a Tennessee regiment. He was subsequently a member of Congress from Tennessee, a member of the Centennial Commission from that State, and postmaster of Nashville. He has long been a citizen of the new State of Washington and is at present city treasurer of Seattle.

As a general proposition I think that the old times in Johnstown were better than the new. If seventy years ago we did not have a homogeneous population we had a population that was perfectly assimilated. Everybody spoke the English language. We had no class distinctions. There were no rich men. There were no long rows of drinking saloons. The Washingtonian temperance movement, which originated in Baltimore in 1840, gave a great blow to intemperance in Johnstown in the early 40s, and it was followed in the same decade by the Sons of Temperance and the Cadets of Temperance. We had two literary societies, each with a large membership of adults, which discussed regularly the leading questions of the day and of other days. There was marked literary taste and much literary culture in Johnstown from 1840 to 1850 and for a few years after 1850. There were no "Sunday morning papers" in those days. If we had no public library there were a few books in almost every home, and it was a common practice for the boys and girls to borrow books from one another. We had in those days two volunteer military companies, composed of our leading citizens. Military encampments, in which these companies participated, took place every year in Johnstown and neighboring towns, and they were great occasions for the boys and for others, as were also the parades which occurred more frequently at home.

The decade from 1840 to 1850 embraced three very exciting Presidential campaigns, which greatly interested the men and women and also the boys and girls of Johnstown—the election of General Harrison and John Tyler over Van Buren and Johnson in 1840, the defeat of Henry Clay in 1844 by James K. Polk, and the election of General Zachary Taylor over Lewis Cass in 1848. It witnessed the annexation of Texas in 1845 and the war with Mexico in 1846, the settlement in 1846 of the controversy with Great Britain over our northwestern boundary, the acquisition of California and other Rocky Mountain and Pacific Coast territory in 1848, the discovery of gold in California in 1848, the Irish famine which so stirred the sympathies of the people of our country in 1846, 1847, and 1848, the passage of the tariff of 1842 and its repeal in 1846, and the great Pittsburgh fire in 1845.

I well remember the passage through Johnstown in 1846 of Philadelphia volunteer soldiers on their way to Mexico and the return of the Cambria county volunteers in 1848. The latter were welcomed and praised at a large meeting in their honor in Levergood's orchard, on which occasion Cyrus L. Pershing delivered an address which I heard. When the Philadelphia volunteers reached Johnstown over the Portage Railroad on their way to Mexico they were distributed in squads among the leading families and given a good supper. I remember standing in awe of these soldiers with their new uniforms and bright muskets.

We had good public schools from 1839 to 1850, which were taught by Samuel Douglass, Orson H. Smith, David F. Gordon, Cyrus L. Pershing, Robert H. Canan, and others, all of whom were well qualified for their work. The schools were ungraded, which was a great advantage over the present system—the younger pupils learning from the recitations of their elders. The classes of boys and girls were required to toe the mark once or twice a day in spelling and reading, and they learned to spell and read correctly because they were taught correctly. Words were divided into syllables and so pronounced, and sentences received proper emphasis. The multiplication table was taught by a whole class reciting it in concert. Instruction in the schoolroom in those days was largely oral; now it is largely lacking in this most desirable feature. That I may not lose the thread and purpose of this letter reading aloud formed a part of the exercises of the Sunday-schools of that time in Johnstown, all of which were conducted in the same spirit and substantially upon the same lines as the one I have briefly described.

Johnstown itself was a beautiful town in my boyhood days. Its surrounding hills were covered with dense forests down to the very margins of the streams which then bounded it on nearly all sides. These streams were not polluted in any way. The water in their channels was as clear as crystal and there was a larger volume of water than now. Fish abounded in them; now there are none. Every spring boys and men organized a fishing party and swept the Stony creek with a brush net, securing hundreds of fish, which were fairly divided and carried home in triumph. In the town, here and there, were many apple orchards which had been planted by Joseph Johns and the other native Pennsylvanians who were its first settlers, and many sycamores, black and white walnuts, and other native trees were still standing. There were many log houses, reminders of the pioneers, and a few brick houses. Every house had a garden attached to it, and there were lilacs, poppies, hollyhocks, sunflowers, and other old-fashioned flowers everywhere. There were but two houses in all "Kernville" in 1840. There was no smoke of mill or factory, but there was little want in any home. Nearly all the business of the town was dependent upon the Pennsylvania Canal and the Portage Railroad, which had given the town its business start only a few years before. As we all know, every town, like every country, has its golden age, and I candidly believe that the golden age of Johnstown was in the ten or fifteen years before 1850. I feel sure that my early friend, W. C. Lewis, will confirm my opinion.

EDWIN AUGUSTUS VICKROY.

PIONEER FARMER, SURVEYOR, AND OLD–TIME MERCHANT
OF JOHNSTOWN. WRITTEN IN 1896. REVISED IN 1910.

EDWIN AUGUSTUS VICKROY, son of Thomas Vickroy,
was born at Alum Bank, Bedford county, Pennsylvania, on
March 8, 1801, and died at his home at Ferndale, a suburb
of Johnstown, on May 1, 1885, aged over 84 years.

Thomas Vickroy was born in Cecil county, Maryland, on
October 18, 1756. His father was Hugh Vickroy, a native
of England, who commanded a vessel plying between Baltimore and Glasgow. His mother was Margaret Phillips, a
native of this country. Thomas was the oldest of eight
children. When he was about 15 years old his father was
lost at sea and very soon afterwards his mother died. In
1772 Thomas moved to Bedford county and soon settled at
Alum Bank. He had learned surveying in Maryland, and
in Bedford county, which then embraced a large part of
Western Pennsylvania, he found abundant opportunities to
practice his profession. He was a noted surveyor in the
last decades of the eighteenth century and the first part of
the nineteenth century. He was so prominent in his profession that he was selected, in conjunction with George
Wood, deputy surveyor of Bedford county, to survey the
town of Pittsburgh into streets, alleys, and lots in 1784.
Vickroy street and Wood street were named in their honor.

Thomas Vickroy was twice married. His first wife was
Elizabeth Francis, who was a half sister of the "sainted
and lovely" Mrs. Emily Ogle, of Somerset, and also a sister
of Mrs. Nancy Williams, of Schellsburg. At her death she
left five children. Mr. Vickroy's second wife was Sarah
Ann Atlee, a daughter of Judge William Augustus Atlee,
of Lancaster, who was a member of the Supreme Court of
Pennsylvania from 1777 to 1799 and was the founder of a
distinguished family. Several of his descendants have been

prominent in the legal and medical professions. The second wife of Thomas Vickroy was a woman of great beauty, who frequently graced the society of Bedford Springs in the old times. Her granddaughter, Mrs. Boyd, of Dublin, Indiana, tells us that she had heard her grandmother say that she had danced in the same set with Theodosia Burr, the beautiful and accomplished daughter of Aaron Burr, on the occasion of Theodosia's last visit to Bedford Springs. She was lost at sea in the winter of 1812–13. After coming to Pennsylvania Thomas Vickroy always lived at Alum Bank. At the time of his marriage to Miss Atlee he had already accumulated considerable wealth. He died on June 9, 1845, in his 89th year, and was buried in the cemetery attached to Dunning's Creek meeting house of the Friends, or Quakers, near Alum Bank. A few years ago a monument was erected over his grave, bearing a suitable inscription commemorating his services as a Revolutionary soldier.

Thomas Vickroy's name is prominently associated with the military movements of George Rogers Clark against the Indians and British in the West during the Revolutionary war. In Albach's *Annals of the West* Thomas Vickroy has left an account of his connection with one of General Clark's expeditions. He says: "In April, 1780, I went to Kentucky, in company with eleven flatboats with movers. We landed on the 4th of May, at the mouth of Beargrass creek, above the Falls of the Ohio. I took my compass and chain along, to make a fortune by surveying, but when we got there the Indians would not let us survey." Mr. Vickroy then gives some details of General Clark's movements against the enemy and adds: "On the 1st day of August, 1780, we crossed the Ohio river and built the two block houses where Cincinnati now stands. I was at the building of the block houses. Then, as General Clark had appointed me commissary of the campaign, he gave the military stores into my hands and gave me orders to maintain that post for fourteen days. He left with me Captain Johnston and about twenty or thirty men who were sick and lame. On the fourteenth day the army returned with 16 scalps, having lost 15 men killed." Joseph, a brother of Thomas Vickroy, was killed in the battle of Germantown.

In 1896 Mrs. Boyd, who was one of the daughters of
Edwin A. Vickroy, wrote us as follows: "When I was a
little girl one of my aunts gave me a strand of beautiful
dark brown hair out of the queue my grandfather sported
in this expedition. Along with the hair of my other grand-
parents I have worn it as a breastpin for 40 years. It was
my first breastpin. I write with it on."

As already stated, Edwin A. Vickroy, in whose memory
this sketch is written, was born at Alum Bank in 1801.
He was the third child of Thomas Vickroy by his second
marriage. Edwin was reared to manhood at Alum Bank.
Here he went to subscription schools, one of which was
taught by Robert Way. Under his father's instructions he
became a skillful surveyor. When about 19 years old he
went to Ohio with Robert Way, the latter remaining there.
Ohio was then "the West," and like "the West" of later
years it presented attractions to young men which were
hard to resist. Edwin clerked in a store in Cincinnati for
two years. While on a visit to Warren county, adjoining
Hamilton county, in which latter county Cincinnati is located, he was fortunate in making the acquaintance of
Judge George Harlan and his family, including his daughter Cornelia, whom he subsequently married. She was born
at the Harlan homestead, near Ridgeville, Warren county,
on August 13, 1806. Her mother's maiden name was Esther
Eulas. The Harlan family has been distinguished in the
history of our country for many generations, contributing
many prominent men to the bench and bar and to the political arena. Judge Harlan came from North Carolina. He
married Miss Eulas while living in Kentucky.

Edwin A. Vickroy and Cornelia Harlan were married at
the Harlan homestead on May 15, 1823, and immediately
afterwards went to Schellsburg, Bedford county, not far from
Alum Bank, where Mr. Vickroy became a country store-
keeper and also postmaster. Schellsburg was then a place
of some importance, as it was located on the leading turnpike which connected the eastern and western parts of
Pennsylvania. But in a short time Mr. Vickroy and his
wife returned to Ohio, near Mrs. Vickroy's old home, where
he again engaged in merchandising, for which occupation

he seems to have always had a strong liking. In this business Mr. Vickroy continued for several years, but, owing to a great fall in the price of pork, in which product he dealt as a merchant, he concluded to return again to Pennsylvania. Those were the days when Ohio had few manufactures to create a home market for farm products. Mr. Vickroy's father transferred to him a beautifully located tract of land on the left bank of Stony creek, near Johnstown, as a home, on which he soon built a two-story log house, weather-boarded, to which he subsequently added a substantial frame addition, with wide porches. This tract had not been improved as a farm. It embraced 160 acres of rich and level meadow and hilly woodland. It was then known as Horseshoe Valley, but Mr. Vickroy soon changed the name to Ferndale. A more charming rural home could not then have been found anywhere. On one side Horseshoe Valley was hedged in by the everlasting hills and on the other side it was bounded by the beautiful Stony creek. The primeval forest which formed a part of the 160 acres was alive with song birds and other birds. Pheasants and partridges, squirrels and rabbits, wild fowl on the bosom of the Stony creek, and an abundance of fish in its waters furnished food for the table. To this home Mr. and Mrs. Vickroy and their three children, Angeline, Louise, and Helen, came in 1831 and there Mr. and Mrs. Vickroy lived the remainder of their days, except about two years spent in Johnstown from 1848 to 1850. Mr. Vickroy at once engaged in farming and at the same time returned to his profession as a surveyor. He also built a saw-mill on the Stony creek and for many years the mill sawed large quantities of lumber from the timber on the farm and from the neighborhood. John Barnes, wagon-maker, of Johnstown, obtained supplies of lumber from this mill for many years.

In a short time Mr. Vickroy could boast a large acquaintance among the people of Cambria and Somerset counties, and because of his general intelligence, his dignified and courtly bearing, and his interest in the public welfare he was popular and greatly respected. He was an ardent friend of common schools and was often chosen a school director. Fruit growing became a special feature of

Mr. Vickroy's farm work, and he soon had an orchard of choice varieties of apples and other fruits, of which he was very proud. Mrs. Vickroy added to the charm of the Ferndale home by her enthusiasm in the cultivation of flowers.

It was not many years after Mr. Vickroy and his family took possession of the Horseshoe farm until he was elected a justice of the peace for Conemaugh township, Cambria county, a position that well fitted in with his profession as a surveyor, because both justices of the peace and surveyors in those days were accustomed to prepare articles of agreement and other documents relating to transfers of real estate. Mr. Vickroy possessed a judicial temperament, and being a remarkably neat and accurate penman he found much to occupy his time for many years both as surveyor and justice of the peace. He was now known as Squire Vickroy. He was at one time elected county surveyor. At first he was a Whig and afterwards a Republican.

But in a wider sense than as a farmer, surveyor, and justice of the peace Mr. Vickroy became known to the people of Cambria and Somerset counties. He was the head of one of the most intellectual families that have ever lived in either of these counties. Mrs. Vickroy was a woman of exceptional intelligence. The Harlan blood ran in her veins. She had read much and thought much upon most of the subjects which then received the attention of thinking men and women, as did also Mr. Vickroy. They were both familiar with the best literature of the day. As their children grew up they shared the literary tastes and acquired many of the intellectual accomplishments of their parents. Books and newspapers were everywhere in the Vickroy home. The slavery question, the Mexican war, the merits and demerits of all the political policies and political leaders of the eventful period from 1840 to 1860 and afterwards, were topics of daily discussion on the Ferndale farm. Visitors to the Vickroy home, which was always one of old-time hospitality, at once found themselves in an atmosphere which aroused and stimulated their own interest in public questions and in literary subjects. In their religious belief Mr. and Mrs. Vickroy were Swedenborgians, to which denomination Thomas Vickroy and his wife also belonged.

And so the years rolled on. The Vickroy home became known throughout Cambria and Somerset counties as a centre of vigorous and independent thought and advanced views upon all subjects which were then attracting public attention. In the meantime the farm was not neglected and the Vickroy apples and other fruits took premiums at the county fairs and at the meetings of the American Pomological Society at Pittsburgh and Philadelphia. Although a man of fine and commanding presence, straight as an Indian, and with the address of a born leader of men Mr. Vickroy never sought political honors. He was, however, always ready to give a reason for the faith that was in him.

About 1848 the longing for an active mercantile life returned to Mr. Vickroy and he opened on Clinton street in Johnstown a general store in a building which he had built on a lot of ground he owned a few feet south of the corner of Washington and Clinton streets. Here he carried on for several years, and with varying fortune, a general store which was well patronized. But the times were hard, very little money was in circulation, the Cambria Iron Works had not been built, and again Mr. Vickroy was constrained to quit storekeeping. Thenceforward to the end of his days he devoted his time to the work of the farm and to his books and the society of his friends, mingling but little with "the madding crowd" and its "ignoble strife."

Mrs. Vickroy died at the Vickroy homestead on August 30, 1880, and Mr. Vickroy died at the old home on May 1, 1885. Each lived to a good old age. Their remains now rest in Grand View cemetery. They were the parents of many children, both boys and girls.

We have mentioned Mr. and Mrs. Vickroy's three oldest daughters, Angeline, Louise, and Helen. Angeline and Louise became teachers, as did also Cornelia, another daughter. All the children, with scarcely an exception, inherited the literary tastes of their parents. Louise established a wide reputation as a writer of graceful poetry and prose. She was a contributor to Grace Greenwood's *Little Pilgrim* and to *Graham's Magazine* in the old days and in later years to *The Century* and other periodicals. In 1860 she delivered a lecture on " The Poets and Poetry of America" before a

large audience in the First Presbyterian church of Johnstown. Her poems were published in book form about the
same time. Mr. Vickroy himself occasionally manifested
a decided talent for poetic expression. Of the daughters
referred to Helen (Mrs. Austin) is the only one now living.
Her home is at Richmond, Indiana. To her and her sister
Louise (Mrs. Boyd) and to another daughter, Laura, now
living at Bryn Athyn, Pennsylvania, we are indebted for
many of the facts contained in this sketch.

As far back as 1850 we remember a bright new school-
house which had been built on the edge of a wooded reser-
vation at the top of Ben's Creek Hill. From this school-
house a winding path led to the Vickroy home through a
dense growth of oaks, maples, hickories, and other forest
trees. There were no intervening houses or cultivated fields
or gardens. Most if not all of the path was on the hillside
of the Vickroy farm itself. The quietness, the restfulness,
the peacefulness, and the sylvan beauty of the whole scene
can never be effaced from the memories of those now living who often wended their way with trooping children
from the attractive school-house down the winding path
to the hospitable home that was built eighty years ago.

" The old road, the hill road, the road that used to go
  Through brier and bloom and gleam and gloom among
    the wooded ways.
  Oh, now that we might follow it as once we did, you know !
  The old road, the home road, the road of happy days."

JOHN ROYER, HUGUENOT.

FROM THE JOHNSTOWN DAILY TRIBUNE OF SATURDAY, MARCH 11, 1899. REVISED IN 1910.

As ALL readers of Pennsylvania history know, the early settlers of William Penn's province were drawn from many European countries. Before the granting of his famous charter in 1681 emigrants from Sweden and Holland and a few Finns and some English had made settlements on the Delaware. After the charter had been granted England and Wales sent large numbers of Quakers and a few Episcopalians; the Continent sent still larger numbers of Lutherans and other Protestants and a few Roman Catholics; Ireland and France also sent a few Roman Catholics, chiefly to Philadelphia, and the North of Ireland sent many Scotch-Irish Presbyterians. Many Protestants came from Germany, France, Switzerland, and Holland. The French, Swiss, and Dutch immigrants have been confounded with the German immigrants because they usually spoke their South German dialect and were of similar religious convictions, and also because they sailed from the same ports and settled in the same localities as the more numerous Germans. They were thus very naturally regarded as forming a part of the great German wave of immigration to Pennsylvania in the eighteenth century. Thousands of these French, Swiss, and Dutch immigrants have left descendants who are known as Pennsylvania Germans but who are not Germans at all.

Most of the French Protestants who emigrated to Pennsylvania came originally from the provinces of Alsace, Lorraine, and Champagne, in Eastern France, although these emigrants had for some time previously, owing to religious persecution at home, lived in more friendly German, Dutch, and Swiss districts. These French Protestants were known as Huguenots. Other Huguenots came from other provinces in France, and these emigrated in large numbers to

New York, South Carolina, and other colonies and provinces of the New World, including Pennsylvania. Some Huguenots had found an asylum in England and Ireland after the Revocation of the Edict of Nantes in 1685 before emigrating to this country.

Among the Huguenot emigrants from Central France to Pennsylvania in the early days were three brothers named Royer. From one of these brothers came John Royer and his descendants. The brothers settled in Lancaster county. The Rev. Mr. Stapleton, of Lewisburg, Union county, an authority upon Huguenot emigration to Pennsylvania, says that Sebastian Royer came to Lancaster county in 1721. We next hear of the family name during the Revolution, when Samuel Royer, the father of John Royer, above mentioned, was a commissary in the Revolutionary army. This Samuel Royer had a brother named Sebastian. In Baird's *Huguenot Emigration to America* I find mention made of Noe Royer, who emigrated to South Carolina between 1681 and 1686. He was the grandson of Sebastian Royer, a native of Tours, the principal town in the province of Tourraine, in Central France. Noe Royer himself was born in Tours. His father's name was also Noe Royer. I mention his ancestry because of the coincidence in the name of his ancestor, Sebastian Royer, and that of the Lancaster immigrant mentioned by Mr. Stapleton, and also of Sebastian, the brother of Samuel Royer. Samuel Royer's wife was Catherine Laubshaw, a native of Switzerland. There are Royers still living in Lancaster county.

John Royer, the subject of this sketch, was born in Franklin county, Pennsylvania, on November 22, 1778. We first hear of him as a clerk at Chambers' Iron Works, about four miles from Loudon, in Path valley, Franklin county. These works embraced Mt. Pleasant furnace and forge, which were built about 1783 by three brothers, William, Benjamin, and George Chambers. The works were burned in 1843. In 1800 John Dunlap built Logan furnace, near Bellefonte, in Centre county, and about 1805–6–7 John Royer and his brother-in-law, Andrew Boggs, operated this furnace under lease from Mr. Dunlap, the firm name being Boggs & Royer.

We next hear of Mr. Royer as the builder, between 1808 and 1810, of Cove forge, in Blair county, then Huntingdon county, Pennsylvania, on the Frankstown branch of the Juniata river, about seventeen miles east of Hollidaysburg. Mr. Royer carried on Cove forge for ten or twelve years. In the spring of 1821 he moved from Cove forge to Williamsburg, in Huntingdon county, and in the same year he was the successful Whig candidate for the lower branch of the Pennsylvania Legislature, defeating David R. Porter, the Democratic candidate, also an ironmaster, who was at the time one of the owners of Sligo forge, on Spruce creek, Huntingdon county, and who was elected Governor of Pennsylvania in 1838 and again in 1841, serving six years. In 1823 Mr. Royer moved from Williamsburg to a point on the Kiskiminitas river below Saltsburg, but on the Westmoreland side of the river, to engage in the manufacture of salt in company with his brother-in-law, Andrew Boggs, who had laid out the town of Saltsburg in the winter of 1816–17 and had given it its name.

From the Kiskiminitas river Mr. Royer moved to Pittsburgh in the spring of 1826, where he opened an iron warehouse. At the end of three years, in the fall of 1829, the Pennsylvania Canal having been completed to Blairsville, Mr. Royer changed his residence to that place, where he acted as the agent for the Pennsylvania and Ohio Transportation Company, goods then being trans-shipped at Blairsville and hauled over the Northern Turnpike to Huntingdon, where they met the eastern division of the canal. Some time in 1832 Mr. Royer moved to Saltsburg, again engaging in the business of making salt, this time at "Boggs's Works," about two miles east of Saltsburg, on the Westmoreland side of the Conemaugh river. In the spring of 1834 Mr. Royer transferred his lease of the above named salt works to George W. Swank and moved to Johnstown, becoming the agent of the Pennsylvania and Ohio line of boats and cars for the transportation of freight and passengers between Philadelphia and Pittsburgh. The Portage Railroad was opened for business in the spring of that year. In this occupation, for which he was admirably fitted, Mr. Royer spent the next eight or ten years, when ill-health compelled him to retire. He was succeeded by William I. Maclay. In the fall of 1838 Mr. Swank also moved his family to Johnstown, where he died on May 29, 1856, at the age of 46 years and a few weeks. He was born in Westmoreland county in 1810 and was my father.

Mr. Royer died at his residence on Washington street, then called Canal street, east of Franklin street, on March 5, 1850, aged 71 years, three months, and thirteen days. His popularity at Johnstown is attested by his election in 1841 as the Whig candidate for the lower house of the Legislature from the district composed of Somerset and Cambria counties. Ill-health prevented him from being a candidate for re-election in 1842 and Major John Linton became the Whig candidate and was elected.

Mr. Royer was a man of more than ordinary ability. His disposition was genial and his manners were courtly. He was a gentleman of the old school. Mrs. Royer, whose maiden name was Jane Boggs, also a native of Franklin county, but of Scotch-Irish ancestry, survived her husband many years, dying at Johnstown, at the home of her son-in-law, Hon. Cyrus L. Pershing, on October 28, 1869, aged 85 years and seven months. She was born on March 13, 1784. The remains of both Mr. and Mrs. Royer now rest in Grand View cemetery. To Mr. and Mrs. Royer were born eleven children, only two of whom arc now living, Sarah Jane, who became the wife of Robert Bingham, and Mary Letitia, who married Hon. Cyrus L. Pershing. We give their names as follows : Catherine, wife of Gen. Edward Hamilton, John Boggs, Samuel J., Theodore, Elizabeth, wife of Dr. Charles D. Pearson, Alfred, Nancy, wife of William L. Shryock, Alexander, Sarah Jane, wife of Robert Bingham, Andrew Francis, and Mary L., wife of Hon. Cyrus L. Pershing. On Sunday, January 22, 1899, Alfred Royer, the last survivor of John Royer's sons, died at the residence of his brother-in-law, William L. Shryock, in Johnstown. Alfred Royer told us that he was the captain of the first train of freight cars that passed over the Portage Railroad from Johnstown to Hollidaysburg. This was in the spring of 1834. For more than fifty years the name of Royer has been prominent in the business and social life of Johnstown.

MAJOR JOHN LINTON.

PREPARED AND PRINTED FOR PRIVATE CIRCULATION IN SEPTEMBER, 1881, AND SINCE REVISED.

IN the latter part of the eighteenth century there lived in County Derry, Ireland, a Scotch-Irish farmer named William Linton, who had three children, William, Mary, and John. John, the youngest, was born in 1773. He was well educated, his studies embracing the higher mathematics, surveying being a branch which he had completely mastered. While still pursuing his studies he became involved in the political troubles which culminated in the Rebellion of 1798 and was forced to fly to America. Landing at Baltimore he obtained employment as a clerk. In a short time he removed to Greencastle, Franklin county, Pennsylvania, where he was first employed as a clerk and afterwards opened a general store, which he kept for several years. Here he met and about 1801 married Ann Park.

The father of Ann Park was Robert Park. In 1794 the Park family emigrated from Ireland to Philadelphia, where the father, who was a teacher of mathematics, soon afterwards died. His widow subsequently married Colonel James Johnston, a surveyor, who had served in the Pennsylvania Line during the Revolution. His home was near Greencastle, to which place the children of Robert Park removed with their mother, and where Ann Park, as we have stated, married John Linton. The remaining children of Robert Park were all married at Greencastle. Elizabeth married John Agnew ; John married Mary Lang, the daughter of Rev. James Lang, a Presbyterian minister ; and Mary married Ninian Cochran, a surveyor of Cumberland, Maryland.

About 1806 John Linton removed with his family to Frankstown, Huntingdon county, now Blair county, where he and his brother-in-law, John Agnew, opened a general store. Soon afterwards the firm was dissolved and John

Agnew removed to Ebensburg, Cambria county, where he resided for several years. One of his daughters, Maria, married Dr. David T. Storm, a physician of Johnstown.

John Linton removed from Frankstown to Johnstown in 1810, where his early education as a surveyor was brought into requisition for the support of his family, conveyancing being in those days part of a surveyor's profession. He surveyed many tracts of land in Cambria county and wrote the articles of agreement and the deeds for their conveyance. In 1811 he was elected one of the commissioners of Cambria county, taking his seat with the board on the 26th of October of that year. The board consisted of James Magehan, Andrew Anderson, and John Linton. In October, 1814, his term of office expired, and in October, 1815, he was re-elected for another term of three years and was qualified on November 6, his associates being John Rhey and James Magehan. John Agnew was elected clerk of the board. The minutes of the board show that John Linton acted with the commissioners for the last time on the 9th of April, 1818. In the minutes of the board, dated August 6, 1818, in the handwriting of Moses Canan, clerk, we read that "David Price and Joseph Burgoon, the commissioners, in conjunction with the court of common pleas, appointed Richard Lewis as commissioner until the next general election, in the place of John Linton, deceased." He died on July 25, 1818, aged 45 years. His remains now rest in Grand View cemetery. Soon after his removal to Johnstown John Linton was appointed postmaster of that place, an appointment which he held until his death. He was succeeded in this office by Shepley Priestley. The first postmaster at Johnstown was John Beaty, who made his first quarterly return on July 1, 1811, but the date of his appointment can not be given, as the records of appointments made during that period have been destroyed by fire. His successor, John Linton, was appointed on July 17, 1811, being the second incumbent of the office.

At the time of his death John Linton resided in the building on the corner of Main and Franklin streets, the site of which was afterwards occupied by the drug store of C. T. Frazer. A few years after the death of her husband Mrs. Linton purchased the upper half of the square of ground lying between Market and Walnut and Main and Locust streets, upon which had been erected a large building that had been used as a public house. This building stood on the site of the residence afterwards occupied by John Dibert. Mrs. Linton died on April 2, 1835, at the age of 54 years. Her remains rest beside those of her husband in Grand View cemetery. Her house was the social centre of Johnstown for many years. She and her husband were Presbyterians in their religious belief. Mrs. Linton was the first person in Johnstown to use bituminous coal as a domestic fuel. She used it in a grate about 1822.

John Linton was the father of six children, all of whom survived him and their mother. Their names were Mary, Robert Park, Jane, John, Eliza, and Louisa. Mary married John Matthews of Johnstown and died in 1855 at Fairfield, Iowa. Her husband, who did not long survive her, had but recently removed to Fairfield. When comparatively a young man Mr. Matthews was elected a member of the State Legislature from the district composed of Somerset and Cambria counties, and upon the opening of the western division of the Pennsylvania Canal in 1830 he was appointed the first collector of tolls in Johnstown. Robert married Phœbe Levergood, daughter of Peter Levergood, the leading citizen of Johnstown. She died in 1842. Robert P. Linton died in March, 1879, after having filled the office of sheriff of Cambria county for three terms, being elected in 1831, 1837, and 1858. His oldest son, Colonel John Park Linton, who died in 1892, was well known as a prominent citizen of the State as well as a lawyer and soldier. Jane married Joseph Chamberlain, a native of Vermont, who had been a resident of Johnstown for several years. He was a civil engineer by profession. He removed to Cleveland about 1846 and died in 1866 at his home in that city. While residing at Johnstown he served one term as one of two representatives of Somerset and Cambria counties in the Legislature. Eliza married Dr. Charles G. Phythian, a native of England but practicing his profession at Johnstown. He removed to Frankfort, Kentucky, in 1844, where his wife died in 1855. One of her children, Robert Lees, has distinguished himself as an officer in the United States Navy, attaining the high rank of commodore. Louisa married S. Moylan Fox, a native of Philadelphia and a graduate of West Point. At the time of his marriage he was engaged as a civil engineer on the Portage Railroad. John, the last to be noticed of the children of John Linton and Ann Park, married Adelaide Henrietta Lacock, the youngest daughter of General Abner Lacock, of Beaver county, on September 1, 1831.

John Linton, the second, after receiving a fair common-school education at Johnstown and Pittsburgh, entered the store of Silas Moore at Ebensburg as a clerk when he was about 16 years old, where he remained about two years, at the end of which time he engaged in business for himself at Johnstown, buying a stock of goods from Shepley and Thomas Priestley and opening a store on Main street. In a few years his old employer, Silas Moore, became a partner with him in his store, when the business was considerably enlarged and the store was removed to the southwest corner of Main and Franklin streets, now " the bank corner." Mr. Moore's interest was soon afterwards purchased by Mr. Linton, who continued the business without a partner for several years, when a partnership was formed with his brother-in-law, Joseph Chamberlain, and the store was removed to the northeast corner of Main and Clinton streets, where a brick store-room was built by the firm. This building was destroyed by the Johnstown flood, at which time it was owned by Jacob Wild. This partnership was continued for many years. During its continuance the firm engaged in various contracts upon the public improvements then in progress in the western part of the State. We remember the sign of this firm, Linton & Chamberlain.

About 1840 John Linton was elected captain of the Conemaugh Guards, a volunteer military company, which he commanded until about the time of his removal from Johnstown to Rochester, Beaver county, in 1853. This company was organized as early as 1835, in which year Governor Ritner, in accordance with the action of the company, commissioned Joseph Chamberlain as its captain. In 1849 Captain Linton was elected inspector of the brigade to which his company was attached, which position conferred upon him the title of major, by which he was ever afterwards known. He served as brigade inspector for several years, and whether as Captain Linton or as Major Linton he was always popular with officers and men.

Political as well as military honors were early conferred upon John Linton. His first vote was cast against Andrew Jackson and he became one of the most active members of the Whig party of Cambria county. In October, 1842, he was chosen a Whig member of the lower branch of the Legislature from the district composed of Somerset and Cambria counties, which was entitled to two members. In the session of 1843, following his election, he secured the partition of the district and the erection of Cambria county into an independent district, entitled to one member. Although the county was Democratic so great was the popularity of John Linton that he was nevertheless re-elected to the Legislature in October, 1843, defeating David Somerville, the Democratic nominee. He was not again a candidate for the Legislature for several years afterwards, but in 1845 he was the Whig candidate for prothonotary, but was beaten by 31 votes, through the defection of a rival aspirant for the nomination. His successful competitor before the people was Joseph McDonald, the regular Democratic nominee. In 1850 Dr. William A. Smith, of Ebensburg, represented Cambria county in the lower branch of the Legislature, and during the session of that year Cambria and Bedford counties were united in one legislative district, entitled to two members. At the election in the fall of that year Dr. Smith of Cambria and John Cessna of Bedford were the Democratic nominees and John Linton of Cambria and Samuel J. Castner of Bedford were the Whig nominees. Cessna and Linton were elected. In 1852 John Linton was a Presidential elector on the Whig State ticket, Winfield Scott and William A. Graham being the Whig candidates for President and Vice President. This was John Linton's last appearance as a candidate for any public office.

In 1845 John Linton, having retired from the mercantile business, formed a partnership with William Huber and Jacob Myers for the manufacture of pig iron, and in that year the firm commenced the erection of Somerset furnace at Forwardstown, in Somerset county, a few miles from Johnstown. The furnace was put in blast in 1846 and in 1847 Mr. Linton disposed of his interest in the enterprise and bought the interest of Peter Levergood in Mount Vernon furnace at Johnstown, which had been built in 1845 and 1846 and was the first furnace at Johnstown. John and Robert P. Linton and John Galbreath became the sole owners of the furnace, under the name of Lintons & Galbreath. This firm was succeeded by Rhey, Matthews & Co.

In 1849 John Linton formed a partnership with George Merriman, of Crawford county, and Colonel Thomas J. Power, of Beaver county, for the construction of one mile of the Pennsylvania Railroad at Johnstown. The work extended from a point just west of the dam in the Conemaugh, near the eastern end of Conemaugh borough, to Cambria City, and was completed in 1850. It embraced the masonry for an iron bridge over the Conemaugh just west of Johnstown. In this year the firm agreed to build about three miles of the Pennsylvania Railroad immediately east of the viaduct over the Conemaugh river east of Johnstown, and extending almost to the village of Summerhill. On the completion of this work in 1853 the firm secured a contract for the construction of a bridge over the Beaver river and about two miles of roadbed below Rochester for the Pittsburgh, Cleveland, and Wheeling Railroad, and Major Linton's presence being required to superintend the work he removed his family to Rochester. The contract was completed in 1855. In this year George Merriman, John Linton, and others took a contract for the construction of eight miles of the Pittsburgh and Erie Railroad. Work on this contract was suspended in 1857, owing to the financial difficulties of the railroad company.

From 1857 until the beginning of the civil war in 1861 Major Linton was not actively engaged in any business. In May, 1861, his old business associate, Colonel Power, who had been placed in charge of the Virginia railroads leading to Washington, sent for him to assist in rebuilding some of the lines which had been destroyed. He was commissioned major by the Secretary of War, Simon Cameron. In this service and in the construction for the Government of steamboat wharves on the Potomac at and opposite to Georgetown Major Linton was engaged until late in the year 1862, when he returned to Rochester. From this time until 1872 he was engaged in various enterprises, after which year he remained in retirement at Rochester.

Major John Linton was born at Frankstown, Blair county, on May 12, 1809, and died at Rochester on December 5, 1894, aged 85 years, six months, and a few days. His wife Adelaide was born at Beaver on June 12, 1808, and died at Rochester on November 1, 1895, aged 87 years, four months, and a few days. They rest in Beaver cemetery.

Ann Park's brother, John Park, came to the wilds of Indiana county in 1795 with Colonel Johnston, who had become his stepfather. In 1798 John Park bought a tract of land on which the town of Marion now stands, and in 1799 he erected a log cabin on the southwest corner of the town, the first house within its limits. Here he died in 1844, at the age of 68 years. Mary Park, who married Ninian Cochran, removed to Johnstown about 1827, after the death of her husband. A daughter, Arabella, came to Johnstown with her mother and a few years afterwards married Selah Chamberlain, a brother of Joseph Chamberlain, and she and her husband were for many years residents of Cleveland. When a young man Selah Chamberlain was a clerk in the store of Linton & Chamberlain. Mrs. Cochran died at Johnstown in 1834. A few years after the death of her husband, Colonel Johnston, the mother of the Park children went to Johnstown to live with her daughter, Mrs. Linton. Here she died on May 31, 1831, aged 82 years.

In No. 2 of Vol. IV of *The Pennsylvania Magazine of History and Biography* (1880) appeared a sketch of General Lacock, prepared by the writer of this sketch. General Lacock, who was a native of Virginia, was frequently a member of the Pennsylvania Legislature, a Representative in Congress from Pennsylvania from 1811 to 1813, and a United States Senator from the same State from 1813 to 1819, and held many other positions of honor and usefulness, dying at his home near Freedom, Beaver county, on the 12th of April, 1837, in his 66th year.

General Lacock is entitled to honorable mention in any detailed reference to the early history of Johnstown. After his term in the Senate had expired he took an active part in advocating the policy of uniting the Delaware and the Ohio by a State line of canals and railroads. From the sketch of his life above referred to we copy the following details : " On the 11th of April, 1825, five commissioners were appointed to make a complete survey of a route for the contemplated improvements, and General Lacock was one of these five, the others being John Sergeant, William Darlington, David Scott, and Robert M. Patterson. General Lacock's commission, signed by Governor J. Andrew Shulze, was dated May 16, 1825. On the 25th of February, 1826, the Legislature authorized the commencement of work on the canal and appropriated $300,000 for its prosecution. General Lacock, who was a member of the board of Canal Commissioners, was appointed by the board the acting commissioner to supervise the construction of the western division of the canal from Pittsburgh to Johnstown. Mainly under his direction this portion of the canal was subsequently built. The first canal boat built or run west of the Allegheny mountains was named the *General Abner Lacock*. It was a freight and passenger packet and was built at Apollo, then Warren, in Armstrong county, about 1827, by Philip Dally, under the auspices of Patrick Leonard, of Pittsburgh."

THE BUILDING OF THE CAMBRIA IRON WORKS.

FROM THE BULLETIN OF THE AMERICAN IRON AND STEEL ASSOCIATION, AUGUST 1, 1888.

IN 1833 George S. King, a merchant of Mercersburg, Franklin county, then 24 years old, came to Johnstown, having heard that it presented opportunities for business that were worthy of his attention. When he saw the town and listened to the sound of the saw and the hammer on every hand he at once concluded that he had been wisely advised and promptly opened a store on Main street. In this and other mercantile enterprises at Johnstown he was very successful during the next few years.

In 1839 and 1840, impressed with the necessity of developing the manufacture of pig iron at or near Johnstown, Mr. King diligently searched for iron ore in its neighboring hills and found it in such quantities and of such satisfactory quality as to encourage him to embark in the business of making pig iron. In 1840 or 1841, at Ross furnace, in Westmoreland county, he tested the ore that he had found in the hills near Laurel run, a few miles below Johnstown. In 1841 Cambria furnace was built on Laurel run by George S. King, David Stewart, John K. Shryock, and William L. Shryock. It was successful from the start. It was soon followed by five other furnaces in Cambria county, as follows: Mill Creek, built by John Bell & Co. in 1845; Ben's Creek, built by George S. King & Co. in 1846; Eliza, five miles west of Ebensburg, on Blacklick creek, commenced by Ritter & Rodgers in 1846 and completed by Ritter & Irvin in 1847; Mount Vernon, at Johnstown, built by Peter Levergood & Co. in 1846 and subsequently owned by Lintons & Galbreath and Rhey, Matthews & Co.; and Ashland, six miles north of Gallitzin, built by Joseph A. Conrad and Hugh McNeal in 1847. All these furnaces have long been abandoned. All used charcoal. The dividing line between Cambria and Indiana counties passed through the stack of Eliza furnace.

Having established the pig iron industry in Cambria county Mr. King turned his attention to the conversion into iron rails of the pig iron that was made at the furnaces near Johnstown or that might be made at new furnaces. The building of the Pennsylvania Railroad, which was completed to Pittsburgh in 1852, convinced Mr. King that the road itself would furnish a market for a large part of the product of a rail mill if one were built at Johnstown. The rail mill that was then nearest to Johnstown was at Brady's Bend, in Armstrong county. Rails were not then made at Pittsburgh. In 1852, therefore, Mr. King visited New York and Boston to explain to capitalists in those cities his scheme for building a rail rolling mill at Johnstown. In the following letter, written at our request, Mr. King gives the details of his eventually successful but always laborious and often disappointing efforts to establish the Cambria Iron Works. Mr. King writes us as follows:

Your letter of May 26th and accompanying copy of your work, *Iron in All Ages*, are at hand, all of which are of much interest and value to me and for which I thank you.

In respect to your request that I give you a history of the origin of the Cambria Iron Works, at Johnstown, I will state that in my effort to do so, for the reason that I am without access to books and memoranda, I can not give dates or enter into the matter as specifically as I would like to do. To properly get at the facts I will go back to my first identification with the iron business, my interest in which finally led to the location and first erection of the Cambria Iron Works, for many years the largest and still one of the most extensive works of their kind in the United States.

Owing to the depressed condition of all business, in consequence of the adoption of the compromise tariff of 1833, a great many of the people being out of employment, as well as myself, I concluded that a means might be found to somewhat change this condition through the iron ore deposits in the hills around Johnstown. After a search of several months I found, in 1839 or 1840, a deposit of ore, and thought it sufficient to justify the erection of a furnace to work it. For the reason that there was but little or no money in circulation my idea was to take the iron out of the ore and trade it for merchandise with which to pay the workingmen and enable them to live.

In the first undertaking I associated with me David Stewart and John K. and Wm. L. Shryock, and I gave the name "Cambria" to our furnace, which we built on Laurel run, about three miles from Johnstown. This being before the day of stone coal for furnace use we used charcoal for fuel. Our first iron was made in 1841. About the latter part of 1843 Dr. Peter Shoenberger, of Pittsburgh, purchased the interest of David Stewart, and in 1844 Dr. Shoenberger and myself purchased the interest of John K. and Wm. L. Shryock, thereby becoming equal owners of Cambria furnace. We sold our pig iron at Pittsburgh.

The tariff of 1842 now being in force and effective, as it better protected the industries of the United States, better times resulted and they justified operators in going into new enterprises and increasing their business. Dr. Shoenberger and I concluded to take advantage of the change, and we built two more new furnaces, Mill Creek and Ben's Creek furnaces, situated about four miles from Johnstown in an opposite direction from Cambria furnace. In these enterprises John Bell was associated with us, remaining so for one or two years, when Dr. Shoenberger and I purchased his interest.

By this time the tariff of 1846 went into operation and it greatly depressed all business, checking enterprise and breaking up much of the iron manufacturing then done in this country. David Stewart, who was formerly associated with me, taking advantage of the recent good times, had built Blacklick furnace, situated about eight miles northwest of Johnstown, in Indiana county. Because of the reductions in duties in the tariff of 1846 Mr. Stewart, like many others, became dissatisfied with the result of his enterprise, and came to us, offering to dispose of it to us, and we purchased it.

We then had four furnaces which we kept alive and in

operation during depressed times for some years, and that, too, with little or no profit to us. In this situation it became a question as to what move we could make in order to perpetuate the business we had engaged in. Dr. Shoenberger advocated the erection of a large foundry, to put our iron into the shape of castings, such as large sugar kettles for the New Orleans market, these and other castings then seeming most in demand.

I advocated the erection of a rolling mill to manufacture railroad iron. Our iron was not adapted for bar iron purposes, and in my opinion was not good for castings, as it was too hard, though in a wrought form I was satisfied that it was good for railroad iron if properly worked, and the result of a trial demonstrated that I was right in this opinion. Finally we agreed upon an effort being made in the direction of organizing a company to erect a rolling mill for the manufacture of railroad iron.

I think that it was in February, 1852, when I left Johnstown to go East to get parties to become interested in the new enterprise. I went first to New York City, and being unacquainted with any one there I was placed at a disadvantage. Among those I could hear of as being most likely to invest in the enterprise was Simeon Draper, a broker, and whom I had heard of quite often. When I called at his office I found him absent, but I presented the matter to his chief business man, George W. Hodges.

Finding but little encouragement in New York I concluded to go to Boston. My first efforts in Boston were not flattering and resulted in my discovering the fountain-head of a concern that I knew something about before. I was taken by a party to the office of an alleged large and wealthy "iron company," and found the office grandly fitted up and well equipped with advertising material, consisting of pamphlets, circulars, etc., one of which was handed to me. It set forth that this "iron company" represented a capital of $500,000 and their works were said to be located near Hollidaysburg, Blair county, where they owned two hundred acres of land and a furnace under construction. I was aware before this that an attempt had been made to build a furnace as mentioned in the pamphlet, and knew all about the matter so well that I got out of that office as soon as possible. I said nothing to them about my matter, nor did I tell them what I knew about theirs.

I next met a party, Mr. Daniel Wilde, to whom I talked about the object I had in view. He called on me at the hotel and we had our second talk, and he proposed that we go and see Mr. John Hartshorn, a broker. We went to his office, I taking with me a schedule of the property Dr. Shoenberger and I intended to put into the business. We saw Mr. Hartshorn and acquainted him with the matter, I laying before him our proposition, which was that Dr. Shoenberger and I should put in our four furnaces, with tools, teams, all the firm's property, except goods· in stores and metal on hand, and twenty-five thousand acres of land, all valued at $300,000, of which we would retain shares in stock to the amount of $100,000 and the rest to be paid to us by the company. Mr. Hartshorn and Mr. Wilde agreed to get up the company within six months' time from date. I then wrote to Dr. Shoenberger to come on to Boston, and on his reaching there he and I signed the articles of agreement as above stated.

Upon me was placed the duty of procuring the charter, and to effect this as soon as possible I went to Harrisburg. In our conversations no mention was made of the name of the company to be organized and the works to be built. Of my own choice and without consulting with Dr. Shoenberger or others I gave the names "Cambria Iron Company" and "Cambria Iron Works." Our capital was placed at $1,000,000 and the works were to be located at Johnstown.

When procuring the charter I found a general law existing that limited the quantity of land to be held by such an organization in one county, and our land not lying in accordance with this provision I went to the Legislature, then in session, and procured the enactment of an additional section to the original law, permitting the holding of lands in more than one county without limit as to quantity. This accomplished and the charter secured I next went to Philadelphia and succeeded in procuring subscriptions of about $30,000 in stock on the part of some merchants with whom I had business relations.

At the expiration of six months our Boston parties had not succeeded as expected and were granted a limit of six months longer to effect their purposes. They transferred their efforts to New York and called on Simeon Draper, whom I had tried to enlist in the matter before I went to Boston. Mr. Draper became a subscriber to the stock and vouched for other subscribers to the amount of $300,000. We then held a meeting to organize the company, resulting as follows: Dr. Peter Shoenberger, president; Simeon Draper, treasurer; George W. Hodges, secretary; and myself, general manager. About this time a change was made in the amount of stock shares to be retained by Dr. Shoenberger and myself, we taking $200,000, instead of $100,000, as first agreed upon, leaving $100,000 to be paid to us in money by the company.

I had before this time conditionally contracted with parties in Johnstown for land which I thought most convenient and best adapted for locating the works, and the company now being organized I immediately secured it and began to erect the rolling mill, four hot-blast coke furnaces, and other buildings, also grading for a coke yard, etc. This was in February, 1853, just one year after I went to New York and Boston to get up the company.

I have herein given you a brief history of the Cambria Iron Company from its origin up to the first work done in the erection of the works, which I think will cover your request as contained in your letter. Very respectfully yours,

GEORGE S. KING.

LEWISTOWN, Fulton County, Illinois, June 14, 1888.

George Shryock King was born at Hagerstown, Maryland, on October 28, 1809, and died at Johnstown on December 8, 1903, aged over 94 years.

HON. DANIEL JOHNSON MORRELL.

FROM THE BULLETIN OF THE AMERICAN IRON AND STEEL
ASSOCIATION, AUGUST 26, 1885.

HON. DANIEL J. MORRELL died at his home in Johnstown on Thursday morning, August 20, 1885, at the age of 64 years and twelve days. Daniel Johnson Morrell was a descendant of one of three brothers who in early colonial days emigrated from Old England to New England. From these three brothers there probably descended all the Morrells and Morrills in the United States to-day. David Morrell, grandfather of Daniel J. Morrell, made his home in Maine considerably over a century ago, and here, in a settlement of Friends, or Quakers, in the town, or township, of Berwick and county of York, was born, one hundred and two years ago, on the farm on which he died eleven years ago, Thaddeus Morrell. When about twenty-three years old he married a neighbor's daughter, Susannah Ayres. They were married on February 17, 1806, and were buried on the same day, June 10, 1874. Ten children were given to this Quaker couple, of whom eight grew to manhood and womanhood. Daniel was the seventh child. He was born on the farm on August 8, 1821.

The childhood and youth of Mr. Morrell were attended by such vicissitudes as are experienced by most boys whose lot has been cast in pioneer homes. His immediate ancestors were true pioneers, whose scanty fortunes had been carved from primeval forests and gleaned from the virgin soil amid many hardships and at the risk of life itself. His father's family wore homespun, woven from threads of flax and wool which had made acquaintance with the family spinning-wheel. When old enough Daniel was taught to assist in the labors of the farm, and when the winter school was in session he was a regular attendant. But the entire time spent by him in the school-room did not exceed two

years. The education thus acquired was, of course, limited to the most elementary studies. The only additional
schooling he ever received was obtained in a course of
study at a commercial college after his entrance upon a
business life. His religious training was such as prevails
among the Friends.

Those citizens of York county who were not engaged
in farming sixty-odd years ago found profitable and needed
employment in some form of manufacturing industry. If
they did not make iron the first settlers of York county
did make it. During the Revolution the colonists had great
difficulty in procuring iron, and extraordinary efforts were
made to supply the want. Many Catalan forges were erected, by means of which malleable iron was obtained directly
from the ore by a single fusion. One of these forges stood
two miles from the farm of David Morrell, and from the
farm itself was taken the ore from which the iron was
made. The grandmother of the boy Daniel used to delight
to tell him how the iron was made by the Catalan process
in the forge that had long been abandoned. Years afterwards, in a distant State, he successfully embarked in the
manufacture of iron and steel on the largest scale and by
the most improved modern processes.

In 1837, when in his sixteenth year, Mr. Morrell left
home and went to Philadelphia, to which city his older
brother David had preceded him. David was engaged in
the wholesale dry-goods trade as a member of the firm of
Trotter, Morrell & Co., which occupied the building now
designated as No. 32 North Fourth street. With this firm
Mr. Morrell was employed as a clerk for five years, until
1842, when the firm was dissolved and he embarked in the
same business for himself, in the same building, his brother
David being associated with him. The business of this firm
was conducted with energy, but with some eccentricity on
the part of David, the older brother, which finally led to
its dissolution. In 1845 Mr. Morrell joined Oliver Martin, a
dealer in fancy dry goods, at No. 28 North Fourth street,
first as a clerk and afterwards as a partner, the firm name
being Martin, Morrell & Co. In 1854 Mr. Martin died and
Mr. Morrell became executor of his estate. Notwithstanding

the death of Mr. Martin the business of the firm continued, and Mr. Morrell's duties kept him constantly engaged until 1855, when his mercantile career ended. He retired with a small capital to assume the management of the Cambria Iron Works, at Johnstown, which had been established in 1853 for the manufacture of iron rails, and which in 1855 passed into the hands of Wood, Morrell & Co. as lessees. This position he retained for nearly twenty-nine years, until January, 1884, when failing health obliged him to retire from all active business.

Down to 1871 the product of the Cambria Iron Works was iron rails solely, in the manufacture of which they had acquired an excellent reputation, but long prior to this year the time had arrived when it became apparent that rails rolled from steel made by the Bessemer process must ultimately displace those made of iron, on account of their greater durability. Mr. Morrell early perceived the coming revolution, and it was largely through his efforts and persistence that the directors of his company were among the first in this country to enter upon the business of manufacturing Bessemer rails. The company commenced their manufacture on July 12, 1871.

During the early part of his mercantile career Mr. Morrell frequently visited the Western and Southern States as a collector, and in this way he obtained a knowledge of the extent and resources of the country which he could not otherwise have acquired. He was a regular attendant for several years upon the lectures of the Franklin Institute, and the time thus spent in a scientific atmosphere was most profitably employed. Attaching himself to the Whig party he became an ardent admirer of its great leader, Henry Clay, and from his speeches he obtained a knowledge of the policy of governmental protection to American industries, of which policy he subsequently became one of the most prominent exponents in the country.

Since 1855 Mr. Morrell had resided continuously in Johnstown and taken an active interest in its growth and prosperity. He might have kept himself aloof from its people and manifested no interest in their welfare, but he chose to regard himself as one of their number and to throw his influence in the scale in behalf of local improvements and an enlarged public spirit. During the Rebellion he greatly aided the cause of the country by encouraging the enlistment of volunteers. Almost every able-bodied employé at the Cambria Iron Works was at some period of the war an enlisted Union soldier. When the war closed his great ability, his patriotism, his intelligent and influential advocacy of the protective policy, and his many sterling qualities of head and heart were recognized by the people of the Congressional district in which he resided, who twice elected him their Representative in Congress—first in 1866 by a majority of 1,219 and again in 1868 by a majority of 1,094. In 1870 he was a candidate for re-election, but was beaten by 11 votes through the defection of a faction of the Republican party in Huntingdon county.

In his first speech in Congress Mr. Morrell uttered the following plea for labor : " The American workingman must live in a house, not a hut; he must wear decent clothes and eat wholesome and nourishing food. He is an integral part of the municipality, the State, and the Nation; subject to no fetters of class or caste ; neither pauper, nor peasant, nor serf, but a free American citizen. He has the ballot, and if it were possible it would be dangerous to degrade him. The country stands pledged to give him education, political power, and a higher form of life than foreign nations accord their laborers, and he must be sustained by higher rates of wages than those of Europe. Our industries operated by American citizens must be freed from foreign interference and organized into a distinct American system, which will exact some temporary sacrifices but result in general prosperity and true national independence. In maintaining diversified industries we utilize every talent, provide a field for every capacity, and bind together the whole people in mutual dependence and support, assuring the strength and security of our Republic." No better definition of the protective policy of this country was ever written.

Upon the organization of the first Congress to which Mr. Morrell was elected, the Fortieth, he was made chairman of the standing committee on manufactures and a member of the standing committee on freedmen's affairs. He retained his chairmanship of the committee on manufactures during the Forty-first Congress, and was also a member of the standing committee on the Pacific Railroad and of the select committee on the decline of American commerce. The feature, however, of his Congressional career with which his name will longest be associated is his introduction on the 9th of March, 1870, of a bill to provide for the celebration at Philadelphia of the hundredth anniversary of American Independence. This bill became a law largely through his persistent advocacy of its propriety and justice, and through the happy effect produced on Congress and the country by his admirably conceived speech of the 14th of December, 1870, in favor of its passage. Upon the organization of the Centennial Commission provided for in the act of Congress the services of Mr. Morrell in securing its creation, and his superior business and executive qualifications, were recognized by his selection as chairman of the executive committee of the commission.

In January, 1878, Mr. Morrell was appointed by President Hayes a commissioner to the Paris Exposition. On Tuesday evening, May 7, 1878, he was tendered a farewell dinner at the Continental Hotel in Philadelphia by leading citizens of the State, including Governor John F. Hartranft, Mayor William S. Stokley, Hon. Morton McMichael, General Robert Patterson, Thomas A. Scott, Henry C. Carey, A. J. Drexel, A. E. Borie, and many others almost equally distinguished. Over one hundred gentlemen sat down to the dinner, which was tendered him " as a complimentary testimonial on the eve of his departure to Europe as a Commissioner from the United States to the International Industrial Exposition at Paris, and in recognition of the services rendered by him to the Centennial Exhibition while he was a member of Congress, and afterwards while filling the arduous and responsible position of chairman of the executive committee of the Centennial Commission during the whole period of its existence." Governor Hartranft presided at the dinner. On May 9, 1878, Mr. Morrell sailed for Europe, returning on the 14th of October, 1878.

On the 6th of March, 1879, Mr. Morrell was elected president of the American Iron and Steel Association. He resigned this office on December 15, 1884, his resignation being accepted and his successor chosen on January 6, 1885. His official retirement from the management of the Cambria Iron Works took place on January 15, 1884, owing to ill-health, as we have already stated.

In 1845 Mr. Morrell married Susan Lower, daughter of Powell Stackhouse, a member of the Society of Friends. His wife and a daughter survive him.* The latter is the wife of Captain Philip E. Chapin, the general manager of the Cambria Iron Works. Mr. Morrell was never blessed with any other children.

The funeral of Mr. Morrell took place on Monday, August 24, and was attended by an immense concourse of his old neighbors and employés. Many friends from a distance were also present. He was buried at Johnstown, amid the scenes of his industrial triumphs and among a people who loved him and will miss him.

---

* Mrs. Morrell died at her home in Johnstown on June 7, 1887. Her daughter, Mrs. Chapin, died in Paris, France, on March 2, 1909.

MAJOR GEORGE NELSON SMITH.

FROM THE JOHNSTOWN DAILY TRIBUNE OF SATURDAY, JANUARY 3, 1891.

DIED, at his residence, No. 2231 Madison Square, Philadelphia, on Monday, December 29, 1890, Major George Nelson Smith, aged 82 years, 6 months, and 10 days.

George Nelson Smith was born at Youngstown, Westmoreland county, on June 19, 1808. His father's name was William Smith and his mother's maiden name was Agnes Nelson. They were natives respectively of the State of Delaware and of Lancaster county, Pennsylvania, and resided, about the beginning of the century, at Elizabethtown, Lancaster county, whence they emigrated to Bedford county and thence to Westmoreland county. Both came of good fighting stock, William Smith's father being at the battles of Brandywine and Germantown and Agnes Nelson's father losing his life from exposure while at Valley Forge.

The father of Major Smith was by trade a cooper, and some years after George was born he went to work making barrels for the salt-makers on the Conemaugh and Kiskiminitas rivers, continuing that occupation for many years. By a sort of evolution George became a keel-boatman on the rivers mentioned and on the Allegheny river, the keel boats taking salt to Pittsburgh. He was a natural waterman, a good swimmer, and fond of the excitement and the dangers of a keel-boatman's life. When the western division of the Pennsylvania Canal was but partly built he left the keel boat for the canal boat, and he enjoyed the honor of having steered the first boat that ran on that division, the *General Abner Lacock.* This was between Warren, now Apollo, and Leechburg in 1829. Entering the service of D. Leech & Co. he became the captain of one of their first packet-boats, the *Pioneer.* Subsequently he had some experience in organizing the company's line on the eastern division of the canal.

When in command of the *Pioneer* an incident occurred which marked a heroic trait of his character. While his boat was spinning along in one of the pools, or dams, of the Kiskiminitas, in 1834, one of the passengers, Mrs. Lovell, the wife of a New Orleans merchant, who also was a passenger, fell overboard. Captain Smith was sitting at an open window at the time. As quick as thought he jumped through the window into the water, and before the boat could be stopped he had safely landed Mrs. Lovell on the bank. This incident has a sequel, as we shall presently see.

In the following year, 1835, Captain Smith and some friends concluded to go West. Taking passage on an Ohio river steamboat they reached Louisville in due time, where they were detained. Here another incident occurred which illustrates again the nobility of Captain Smith's character. Walking along the levee he noticed a woman who was surrounded by two or three little children and a few household goods and was in great distress. Inquiry revealed the fact that her husband had been killed in a Louisville factory and that she was anxious to return to her home at Pittsburgh, but her funds were wholly inadequate to meet the necessary steamboat charges. Captain Smith at once paid her steamboat fare and that of her children to Pittsburgh, and also paid the steward of the boat for their entertainment until their destination should be reached.

But this act of generosity emptied Captain Smith's always lean purse. Abandoning his companions he shipped as a deck hand on a steamboat that was going to New Orleans, at which place he safely arrived. Here he renewed his acquaintance with Mr. Lovell, who gave him a letter of introduction to David G. Burnet, one of the leaders of the struggling Texan Republic, Captain Smith's adventurous spirit and his manly sympathies combining to direct his steps toward the Lone Star State. Arriving in Texas he enlisted as a soldier in the Texan army, and at the battle of San Jacinto, on April 21, 1836, he had the pleasure of contributing to the defeat of the Mexican army and of participating in the capture of Santa Anna himself. For his services in the Texan Revolution he was afterwards granted a large tract of land in Texas, but he did not derive any

benefit from this donation, owing to the undeveloped condition of the country.

Leaving Texas in 1836 or 1837 Captain Smith was induced by friends to locate in Kentucky and he became a
contractor in the building of the Louisville and Nashville
Turnpike. While thus engaged he married Miss Rebecca
G. Mudd, of Green county, Kentucky. This was in 1839.
Soon afterwards he concluded to return to Pennsylvania,
and in 1840, through the kind offices of one of his early
friends, Captain Samuel D. Karns, he was appointed to a
clerkship in the office of the collector of tolls on the Pennsylvania Canal at Johnstown, the collector, Major James
Potts, being a brother-in-law of Captain Karns. Captain
Smith was at this time a good penman and a good accountant, although he had received a very imperfect education when a boy. Thenceforward until 1861 he was an
active and influential citizen of Johnstown. It was not
born in him to be quiet anywhere, or to be a laggard in
matters of public interest. He was a born leader of men
and not a follower.

After Major Potts retired from the position of collector
of tolls in 1842, if not, indeed, before this event, Captain
Smith's old love of the water returned, and he successively
became the owner and captain of two portable boats on the
main line of the Pennsylvania Canal and its railroad connections, named the *Excelsior* and the *San Jacinto*. Dr.
Campbell Sheridan can tell some interesting stories about
the *Excelsior*. But, like all of Captain Smith's business enterprises, he made but little money out of his boating ven-
tures, and in 1846, when the Mexican war broke out, we
find him attached as a sutler's clerk to the First Regiment
of Pennsylvania Volunteers, commanded by Colonel Samuel
W. Black, Captain Samuel D. Karns being the sutler. We
may be sure that it was through no fear of personal harm
that Captain Smith did not occupy a different position in
the regiment. He remained in Mexico with General Scott's
army until the war closed, often exposed to danger and
often participating in movements against the enemy. In a
skirmishing expedition he was wounded in the left leg,
and thereafter he walked with a slight limp.

After returning to Johnstown late in 1847 or early in 1848 Captain Smith was for a time the manager of Ben's Creek furnace, near Johnstown, immediately preceding, we think, that accomplished gentleman, William C. McCormick. This position he held for only a short time. Our recollection is that he next embarked on an active political career by assuming the editorship and the publication of the Democratic paper at Johnstown which had previously been published by Henry C. Devine and was called *The Cambria Transcript*. It was late in 1849 when Captain Smith took charge of this paper, the name of which he changed to *The Mountain Echo*. In the spring of 1853, after encountering some vicissitudes, a "new series" of the *Echo* appeared, the number of columns being enlarged and the name being also enlarged to *The Allegheny Mountain Echo and Johnstown Commercial Advertiser and Intelligencer*. In the meantime Captain Smith had been appointed cargo inspector at Johnstown and had become a Democratic leader and a man of mark among Democrats throughout the State. He could write a good editorial article on almost any subject; he could make a very fair speech on almost any question; he was a good vocalist and delighted to sing political and patriotic songs; he was the author of at least one notable patriotic song; he was a good fiddler; he could tell a story; he was good company anywhere; and he was a man of fine appearance. His physical and moral courage were well known, and his generous and chivalrous nature was just as well known.

After awhile, in October, 1856, while still editing the *Echo*, Captain Smith was elected by the Democrats to the lower house of the Pennsylvania Legislature and was consecutively elected a second and third time to the same body. In the winter of 1856 and 1857 he joined with other Democrats in refusing to vote for John W. Forney, the Democratic caucus nominee for United States Senator, and this action defeated that gentleman and resulted eventually in the election of Simon Cameron. Captain Smith and his associates, seven in all, voted for Henry D. Foster. They refused to go into the caucus because President-elect Buchanan had written a letter virtually dictating Colonel For-

ney's nomination. During his last term in the Legislature
Captain Smith's popularity with his fellow-Democrats was
shown in his election as Speaker *pro tem.*, to fill a vacancy
caused by the ill-health of the regular Speaker. At the
close of the session he was presented with a silver tea-set.
Engraved upon the pitcher there was the following inscription: " George N. Smith, of Cambria County, elected unanimously Speaker *pro tem.*, House of Representatives of Pennsylvania, Session of 1858."

   In 1860 Captain Smith, who was still editing the *Echo*,
was selected as a delegate to the Charleston Convention of
that year. He went to Charleston as a friend of John C.
Breckinridge and supported his nomination for the Presi-
dency until he became satisfied that the friends of Breckinridge were bent upon disunion, when he joined the forces
of Stephen A. Douglas. It will be remembered that the
convention broke in two at Charleston and that the two
wings afterwards met separately at Baltimore, each wing
nominating its favorite. Captain Smith attended the Douglas Convention as a delegate and voted for him. The an-
nexed correspondence will be read with interest.

BARNUM'S HOTEL, Baltimore, June 26, 1860.
   HON. JOHN C. BRECKINRIDGE. My Dear Friend : I trust in God you
will not suffer the evil advice of designing men to cause you to pursue
a course that will destroy the party and ruin yourself. Should you accept the nomination of the Seceders' Convention it will be fatal to the
party and ruinous to you. I beseech you to consider well the step you
are about to take. Evil must assuredly follow acceptance. Your Sincere
Friend,   ——   G. NELSON SMITH.

WASHINGTON CITY, June 28, 1860.
   G. NELSON SMITH, ESQ., Johnstown, Pa. My Dear Sir : I have your
letter and appreciate the motives that dictated it. My course has been
surrounded by difficulties for which I was wholly blameless. We must
each pursue what seems to be the path of duty. Let it not disturb the
personal friendship I am happy to cherish for you. With good wishes,
I remain Your Friend,   JOHN C. BRECKINRIDGE.

   The break-up at Charleston extended to the Democratic
party of the whole country, and the Cambria county Democrats at once took sides with either Breckinridge or Douglas. In the fall of 1860 there were four candidates for the
General Assembly, the Republicans nominating Alexander
C. Mullin, the Breckinridge Democrats Michael Dan Mage-

han, the Douglas Democrats Captain Smith, and the New County party Major James Potts. Mullin was elected.

The split in the Democratic party did not extend to the State politics of Pennsylvania. Henry D. Foster was the Democratic nominee for Governor but was defeated by Andrew G. Curtin. Captain Smith presided over the convention which nominated his old friend, General Foster. This was his last appearance in the Democratic politics of Pennsylvania. The war came soon afterwards, justifying his judgment of the purposes of the Southern Democrats at Charleston. It brought changes in the political as well as personal relations of Captain Smith and other Democrats.

Soon after the close of the political campaign of 1860 Captain Smith's old friend, Samuel D. Karns, invited him to engage with him in an oil speculation in West Virginia. In April, 1861, after the firing on Fort Sumter, the West Virginia Confederates drove them out of the State.

Returning to Johnstown Captain Smith closed the *Echo* office and sought a position with the Union army. He was an intense lover of his country and its flag and his patriotic ardor would not permit him to remain in quiet Johnstown when that flag was insulted. His lameness prevented him from enlisting as a soldier in its defense, but he was appointed quartermaster of the second brigade of Fitz John Porter's division, serving in this capacity, with the rank of captain, until 1862, when he was appointed an assistant paymaster in the army with the rank of major, in which position he served until the close of the war in 1865, being all the time attached to the Army of the Potomac. His two oldest sons, Robert Emmet and Montgomery Pike, were private soldiers in the same army. Montgomery was wounded in the last day's fighting in front of Petersburg, dying in 1870, his wound contributing to his death.

If Major Smith had now gone back to Johnstown among his old friends he would have done wisely, but he had parted with the *Echo* at the breaking out of the Rebellion and moved his family to Baltimore in 1864 while still in the Government service, and when the war closed he felt that there was nothing to take him to Johnstown. This mistake he often regretted afterwards. In the spring of 1866 he tried farming in Virginia, in the neighborhood of Washington, but this experiment failing he sought and secured a clerkship in the custom house at Philadelphia, where he remained until 1869, removing his family to that city soon after his appointment, where he ever afterwards resided until his death. From 1869 forward Major Smith experienced nothing but bad luck. He tried many honorable ways of making a living, including several visits to Texas in the interest of various mining enterprises. For a number of years before his death he lived a life of retirement and almost of seclusion, but still using his pen in many ways and never for one moment losing his interest in public affairs. In 1878 his wife died.

Major Smith's mother was a devout Methodist and his father was a non-professor of religion. The major himself never, until about the time of his wife's death, appeared to take any interest in religious matters. Mrs. Smith was all her life a Roman Catholic and she reared her children in that faith. A short time before her death the major united with the same church, and ever afterwards he was one of its most faithful adherents and a regular attendant upon its services. Major Smith and his wife were the parents of eight children, all born at Johnstown, two of whom we have mentioned.

The remains of our old friend were taken on Friday morning from his residence to the church of St. Charles Borromeo, at Twentieth and Christian streets, and thence to Georgetown, D. C., where they will find a last resting-place in Holy Rood cemetery. The remains of his wife will be taken to Georgetown and laid beside those of her husband.

We have in the foregoing lines traced the career of a really remarkable man. Courage and generosity were the traits by which he was best known to the generation to which he belonged, but he had many other noble qualities. No truer friend ever lived and no more manly opponent. He was kind to those who most needed kindness, the poor and the lowly, and he spurned and contemned alike the insolence of power and the arrogance of wealth. He was an intense lover of his country. He was public spirited. He was a good friend to Johnstown in the days when his

voice and vote could influence its destiny. He passed
through the Legislature the bill incorporating the Johnstown Water and Gas Company and the bill dividing Johnstown into four wards. He was a charter member of the
Johnstown Division of Sons of Temperance.

Of his generous and chivalrous nature we could give
many illustrations in addition to those already mentioned.
While president of the select council of Johnstown in 1858
he was called upon one day to act as burgess and to im-
pose fines upon two men for fighting. One man promptly
paid his fine but the other man being impecunious Captain
Smith paid his fine for him rather than send him to the
lock-up. We personally know of two cases in Johnstown
in which he saved the lives of drowning men by plung-
ing into the water and risking his own life, once into the
canal upon a night of pitchy darkness. One day, when
the Pennsylvania Canal was in all its glory, some heart-
less boatmen took from a boat which had just arrived at
Johnstown a sick woman and her helpless children and
placed the mother on a bench at one of the wharves.
This poor woman was sick with Asiatic cholera. Captain
Smith heard of what had been done, and after vainly endeavoring to secure a lodging place for the sick woman
he took her and her children to his own house, where she
soon afterwards died. That other noble-hearted gentleman,
William Orr, the undertaker, and two good women properly
cared for her remains and she was decently buried. The
children were restored to their father.

DR. WILLIAM ANTHONY SMITH.

FROM THE JOHNSTOWN DAILY TRIBUNE OF TUESDAY, NOVEMBER 1, 1887.

DR. WILLIAM A. SMITH died at his residence in Phila- delphia on Sunday morning, October 30, 1887.

Dr. Smith came of honored and even distinguished line- age. His great-grandfather, William Smith, D.D., a native of Aberdeen, in Scotland, was a clergyman of the Episcopal Church in Philadelphia before the Revolution and for many years afterwards. His prominence in the church and among the learned men of Philadelphia was such that he was ap- pointed the first provost of the University of Pennsylvania, a position which he filled most acceptably for many years. He married a Miss Moore, of the vicinity of Philadelphia, whose family was one of the most aristocratic and worthy in the Province of Pennsylvania. Their oldest son was William Moore Smith, who became distinguished as a Philadelphia lawyer and diplomat, having been sent by Washington on a protracted mission to England, the duties of which he discharged with tact and good judgment. His wife was a Miss Rudolph, a descendant of one of the early Swedish settlers on the Delaware. Their oldest son was General William Rudolph Smith, who married a Miss Anthony, of Philadelphia. These were the parents of Dr. William Anthony Smith.

Provost William Smith was not only an eminent divine and a successful instructor of young men but he was also a shrewd man of affairs. He early foresaw the possibilities of Central and Western Pennsylvania, and patented many tracts of land in the Juniata valley and as far west as the territory now embraced in Cambria county. Among his acquisitions was the site of the town of Huntingdon, in Huntingdon county, which he surveyed into town lots in 1767, naming the town after Lady Huntingdon, of England, who had been a liberal patron of the University of Pennsylvania. To the town of Huntingdon General William R. Smith came from Philadelphia early in the nineteenth century to practice his profession as a lawyer, and here, on the 13th of November, 1809, was born his oldest child, William A. Smith. If William A. Smith had lived just two weeks longer he would have been 78 years old.

When still a boy William A. Smith lost his mother by death and the Huntingdon home was temporarily broken up. He was sent to live with his grandmother in the vicinity of Philadelphia, and in the schools of that city and its neighborhood he received a good elementary education, which was subsequently completed at Huntingdon, after his father's second marriage and the re-establishment of his home at that place. About the time William's literary and classical studies were completed his father removed to a farm in the vicinity of Bedford but continued to practice his profession in the courts of Huntingdon, Bedford, and Cambria counties until his removal to Wisconsin in 1838. William went with his father to the farm and for a short time helped to manage it. Before he was twenty years old, however, we find his love of books asserting itself and he became a medical student at the office of Dr. Watson, of Bedford. His medical studies were subsequently completed at the University of Pennsylvania, which conferred upon him the degree of doctor of medicine in 1832.

Dr. Smith commenced the practice of his profession at Bedford, where he remained only a short time, thence going to Somerset, where he opened an office and remained until after the town was devastated by a great fire in the fall of 1833, his own office being burned. From Somerset he removed to Ebensburg, Cambria county, where he at once entered upon an extensive practice, which he retained until his removal to Philadelphia in 1858, subject to occasional interruptions, which will presently be explained. At Somerset Dr. Smith formed the acquaintance of Jeremiah S. Black, and a strong intimacy existed between the two men until the death of Judge Black a few years ago. The two young men roomed together at Somerset.

In 1841 Dr. Smith was married to Miss Rebecca C. Bellas, of Milton, Pa., a cousin of Mrs. Dr. Rodrigue, of Ebensburg. Four sons were born to this union. In 1858 Dr. Smith removed with his family to Philadelphia, the home of his immediate ancestors, that he might give his children the advantages of a liberal education. To do this he temporarily abandoned the practice of his profession and became an inspector in the Philadelphia custom house. In 1861 his wife died, and in 1862 he entered the Government service as an army surgeon, continuing in this position until 1866, when he was mustered out. Soon after entering the army he was captured at Savage Station, while serving under McClellan, but was soon afterwards released. His oldest son, William Bellas Smith, born in 1842, was employed in the medical service during the war. He died and was buried at sea in 1866 while returning home from the Southwest, where he had for some time been stationed. He was a young man of particularly winning ways and of very bright promise. His father never recovered from this blow.

Soon after retiring from the army Dr. Smith was appointed to a responsible position in the office of the prothonotary of the Supreme Court of Pennsylvania for the eastern district, which position he filled most creditably for about twenty years until attacked by his last illness.

General William R. Smith was very prominent in the military affairs of the Juniata valley, and his son, the doctor, inherited his military tastes. Soon after he settled in Ebensburg he was chosen captain of the Cambria Guards. This office he held for ten years. Many old residents of Ebensburg still refer to him as Captain Smith. He took great interest in the welfare of his company, and it was largely owing to his zeal and popularity as its commanding officer that it was ready with full ranks to go to Mexico in the spring of 1847. The doctor was himself, however, prevented from going with his men, but his interest in military matters never suffered any abatement to the last year of his life. When his company returned to Ebensburg in 1848 with broken ranks he delivered an address of welcome. He was a sincere and ardent lover of his country, and her history and achievements were to him a constant delight.

If Dr. Smith was a born soldier he was also a born politician of the better class. He was an ardent Democrat when he cast his first Presidential vote for Andrew Jackson in 1832, and he remained a Democrat all his days. He and his father were warm friends of Governor David R. Porter, who was their fellow citizen at Huntingdon, and soon after the Governor's first election in 1838 he appointed Dr. Smith to be prothonotary of Cambria county, succeeding Dr. David T. Storm. Dr. Smith held this office for several years. He was an elegant penman, and he made a capable and obliging court officer.

In 1848 John Fenlon, a Whig, was elected to the lower branch of the State Legislature, defeating Colonel John Kane, a Democrat. In 1849 the Whigs again ran Mr. Fenlon for the same office, but he was defeated by Dr. Smith, who accordingly served in the Legislature of 1850. In the fall of that year Dr. Smith was again the nominee of his party for the same office, but this time he was himself defeated by John Linton, Whig. In 1854 the doctor was the Democratic candidate for the lower house of the Legislature, but was defeated by George S. King, the Whig candidate.

During his residence in Ebensburg Dr. Smith was frequently chosen a delegate to State conventions and was otherwise honored by his party. He was, in fact, one of the leaders of the party as long as he remained a citizen of Cambria county. It was largely through his personal influence that the new-county scheme was defeated at Harrisburg while Mr. King, its champion, was in the Legislature. He was always ready with a forcible speech in defense of the regular Democratic ticket. After his removal to Philadelphia he maintained to the last his intimate personal relations with party leaders, who always respected his judgment and were often warmed by his enthusiasm.

The foregoing are the leading facts in the long and useful life of one of the worthiest citizens Cambria county has ever had. They leave his character undescribed, and a man's character is, after all, the principal part of the man. He was always willing to extend any favor or courtesy that was in his power to grant. As a physician he answered many calls without hope of reward, and this often at much personal sacrifice in the bitter winters of Northern Cambria.

His fidelity to his friends was a marked trait, and his attachment to Huntingdon, the home of his childhood, and to Ebensburg was pathetic in its tenderness.

Among Dr. Smith's varied attainments was a cultivated literary taste. He was a great reader and a vigorous writer. The newspapers of Bedford and Cambria counties contained many well-written contributions from his ready pen in the days before the civil war. While residing in Ebensburg he was universally accepted as an authority in all literary matters, and upon historical subjects particularly he was a veritable cyclopædia. His literary style was forcible, direct, and elegant. While residing in Philadelphia he became an active member of St. Andrew's Society, and after he was 65 years old he prepared and published elaborate historical sketches of its first two presiding officers, Dr. Thomas Graeme and Lieutenant Governor James Hamilton, both ante-Revolutionary characters. These two literary productions are so well written and so perfect in all literary essentials that they alone entitle their author to an honorable place among Pennsylvania's historical writers.

The remains of our old friend were buried in St. Peter's churchyard, at the corner of Third and Pine streets, Philadelphia, on Tuesday afternoon, the 1st of November, 1887.

Dr. Smith's father, William Rudolph Smith, was born at La Trappe, Montgomery county, Pennsylvania, on August 31, 1787, and died at Quincy, Illinois, on August 22, 1868. In 1803 he accompanied his father to England as his private secretary, studied law in the Middle Temple, and on his return home in 1808 was admitted to the bar of Philadelphia. He removed to Huntingdon county in the following year and in 1811 he became deputy attorney general of Cambria county. He subsequently removed to Bedford county. Removing to Wisconsin in 1838 he took an active part in its affairs until his death.

JUDGE JAMES POTTS.

WRITTEN IN 1891 AND PRINTED IN PAMPHLET FORM FOR PRIVATE CIRCULATION.

ON August 8, 1891, the old citizens of Johnstown and more than forty members of the bar of Cambria county laid to rest in Grand View cemetery the remains of Hon. James Potts, who died at Oil City, Venango county, on Thursday, August 6, 1891. He was born at Butler, Pennsylvania, on August 31, 1809, and was consequently at the time of his death almost 82 years old.

James Potts was the son of John Potts, a native of the North of Ireland. His mother's maiden name was Jane Karns, who was also of Scotch-Irish extraction. Both families were not only among the first settlers of Western Pennsylvania but they were also long prominent in the social, business, and political affairs of that part of our State. John Potts, the father of James Potts, was one of the pioneer settlers of the town of Butler. He was a merchant. He was also an active and influential politician. He represented Butler county in the Legislature at a very early day and also held the offices of county treasurer and county commissioner. Two of his sons, George and James, were also politicians from their boyhood. The father was a disciple of Thomas Jefferson and his sons were Democrats all their days. The Karns family was divided in its political allegiance. Two members of this family, William and Samuel D. Karns, brothers, were prominent in the councils of the Democratic and Whig parties respectively.

The town of Butler was mainly settled by brainy, enterprising, and cultivated families, who were nearly all of Scotch-Irish origin and Presbyterian in their religious faith. Among a people of such characteristics and antecedents James Potts grew up. He lacked no advantages which churches, schools, good health, a comfortable home, ambitious parents, and superior social surroundings could give. He lived in an intellectual and social atmosphere that was wholesome and elevating. Intended for one of the liberal professions he became a student of Jefferson College when he was about 17 years old, and he almost completed the regular four years' course. Owing to some accidental occurrence he did not graduate, but he obtained a good knowledge of Latin and Greek and the higher mathematics and some knowledge of Hebrew. He was a great reader of history while at college and ever afterwards. He was born with decided literary tastes, and at college these tastes had opportunity for healthy development. When yet a young man he had read much good literature, was a writer of good English, and was a ready and impressive public speaker.

Leaving college about 1829 or 1830 James Potts appears to have not immediately entered upon the study of a profession, as we hear of him a few years later as a student of law with his early friend and playmate, Samuel A. Purviance, of Butler, who afterwards became noted for his legal attainments and his political prominence. James Potts did, however, push his way to the front of Butler county politics soon after leaving college, and with such success that when he was 25 years old he was postmaster of Butler. About the time when he was appointed to this political office he was elected captain of an infantry company, the Butler Blues, a volunteer military organization, and a little while later he was elected major of the battalion to which his company was attached. In 1837, after he had commenced the study of law, he was appointed one of the clerks of the Pennsylvania Constitutional Convention of that year, of which some of the most eminent men of the State were members. Here his opportunities for increasing his political acquaintance and forming political friendships were most excellent, and he at once attained a high standing among the Democratic leaders of Pennsylvania.

On the 2d day of October, 1838, James Potts and his cousin, Margaret Jane Karns, were married at Pittsburgh by the Rev. James Prestly. Mrs. Potts's father's name was James Elliott Karns. During the following winter the canal commissioners, under the administration of Governor

David R. Porter, appointed James Potts, who had first been Captain Potts and was now Major Potts, collector of tolls at Johnstown, on the main line of the public improvements of the State, succeeding Frederick Sharretts, a Whig. Soon after his appointment Major Potts visited Johnstown for the first time, and in March, 1839, when less than 30 years old, he entered upon his new duties and set up housekeeping in the official residence of the collector, attached to the collector's office on Canal street, now Washington street. Major Potts continued as collector of tolls for five years, or until 1844, when he was succeeded by A. W. Wasson, of Erie, who was in turn succeeded a few years later by Obed Edson, of Warren. During a large part of Major Potts's term as collector he had as his clerks George Nelson Smith, Campbell Sheridan, and Cyrus L. Pershing, all well known to the old citizens of Johnstown.

Upon coming to Johnstown in the spring of 1839 Major Potts and his wife at once became a positive and beneficent social force in their new home. They were a handsome couple, tasteful in dress, courtly in manner, fond of social gatherings where gentility counted for something, exceedingly hospitable in their own elegantly furnished home, regular attendants at church, and possessed of many polite accomplishments as well as a generous income apart from the emoluments of the collector's office. Mrs. Potts was a woman of rare grace and of queenly presence, of most winning ways, cheerful and hopeful under all circumstances, devoted to her home, ever ready to make others happy, the possessor of a mind cultivated by much reading and contact with well-read and well-bred people—a lady, in brief, of exalted character. She died on August 9, 1879, in Johnstown, living there all her married life. She was the mother of eight children. Her oldest daughter Jane lost her life in the Johnstown flood of 1889.

When Major Potts surrendered the collector's office to his successor he opened an office on Clinton street for the practice of law so far as this could be done without his having previously been admitted to the bar. He had not completed his legal studies when he came to Johnstown, but when the whirligig of politics threw him on his own resources he resolved not only to make Johnstown his permanent home but to rely upon the practice of law for a livelihood. To comply with the court regulations before applying for admission to the bar he nominally became a student with Hon. Moses Canan, then the only lawyer in Johnstown, and on the 7th of October, 1846, he was formally admitted as a member of the Cambria county bar. He at once entered upon an active and lucrative practice, in which he continued until advancing years and declining health caused him to virtually retire from the further practice of his profession. On June 11, 1850, when on a visit to his old home in Butler, he was admitted as a member of the Butler county bar. For about three years, beginning with 1850, he was the senior member of the law firm of Potts & Kopelin. Abram Kopelin had studied law with Major Potts and was a bright and promising student. He afterwards became one of the most distinguished members of the Cambria county bar. Major Potts never had any other law partner.

At the time of his death Major Potts was the oldest in years of all the members of the Cambria county bar, but there survived him two members who were engaged in practice before he had been admitted. Hon. John Fenlon was admitted on July 3, 1837, and General Joseph McDonald on April 3, 1844. For these dates I am indebted to Hon. George M. Reade, of Ebensburg, who completed his legal studies with Potts & Kopelin.

As early as 1850 an active agitation had commenced in the southern part of Cambria county in favor of the establishment of a new county, with Johnstown as the county-seat, and in 1854, after the election of George S. King to the Legislature, this movement, with which Mr. King earnestly sympathized, took shape in the preparation of a bill which provided for the organization of a new county. The measure failed before the Legislature, but the agitation was again fiercely renewed in 1860, when Major Potts, who had from the first been one of its principal promoters, became the candidate for the Legislature of what was known as the New County party. He was defeated after a most animated canvass, which has probably never been surpassed in intensity in Cambria county. Then the war came, but a few years after it closed the new-county movement was again renewed with great energy, this time, however, taking the form of a proposition to remove the county-seat from Ebensburg to Johnstown. In 1870 Captain H. D. Woodruff, of Johnstown, ran as a candidate for the Legislature on this issue, but was defeated by a small majority. It had previously been proposed to establish at Johnstown a district court which should include within its jurisdiction Johnstown and some neighboring towns and townships. This scheme was so far successful that in 1869 it was approved in an act of the Legislature and the court was duly established, the judges of the Cambria county courts officiating as judges of the district court. Subsequent legislation provided for the election of all district court officers by the citizens of the district, but before an election could be held the offices were filled by appointment of the Governor, Major Potts being appointed president judge by Governor Geary in 1871. He was subsequently elected to this position. Several sessions of the new court were held with Judge Potts on the bench. But the court, which had at first been eagerly desired, soon fell into disfavor because by the terms creating it it partook too much of the character of a police court. There was much legislation concerning it and much litigation. In 1874 Judge Potts was defeated as a candidate for re-election to the judgeship, and in 1875 the Supreme Court of the State decided that the act creating the district court was unconstitutional. This ended the new-county and county-seat agitation which had existed for a quarter of a century.

Soon after coming to Johnstown Major Potts took an interest in its military affairs. There had existed for a number of years a volunteer infantry company called the Conemaugh Guards, of which Joseph Chamberlain, John K. Shryock, and John Linton were successively captains. About 1841 a rival company was organized, called the Washington Artillerists, of which Peter Levergood, Jr., was elected captain. He was succeeded by George W. Easly, and about 1842 Collector Potts was elected captain, a position which he held for many years. The name of the company had in the meantime been changed to Washington Grays. The Grays were often on dress parade and with the Conemaugh Guards they participated in many encampments. Those were stirring times for a country town. Major Potts was a good drill officer. At the beginning of the Rebellion he took delight in drilling Johnstown volunteers for the Union army. I may here recall the interesting fact that James Potts played the drum on the 3d day of June, 1825, upon the occasion of Lafayette's reception by the people of the town of Butler, and that the fifer whom he accompanied with his drum was a Revolutionary soldier named Peter McKinney, who had played the fife at Bunker Hill in 1775, just fifty years before. In our old friend we have had a link to connect the present generation with Revolutionary days.

In 1840, not long after Major Potts came to Johnstown, the Washingtonian temperance movement was started, and in this movement he took an active interest, attending and addressing the meetings which were held in 1840 and 1841, and perhaps in 1842, in the various churches of Johnstown, and aiding greatly by his earnestness and ability in obtaining signers to the Washingtonian pledge. The Washingtonian movement in Johnstown was soon followed by the organization of the Juvenile Temperance Society, and the credit of originating and perfecting this organization belongs wholly to Major Potts. It lasted for two or three years, and did great good in starting many Johnstown boys in the right path. Subsequently Major Potts assisted in organizing the Johnstown Division of Sons of Temperance and its companion the Cadets of Temperance. All his days he was a consistent and earnest temperance man. His influence in Johnstown in behalf of temperance was a marked feature of his useful life.

But Major Potts was active in other good works in Johnstown for many years after he became one of its citizens and at a time when men of capacity and courage were greatly needed. It will surprise many who read these lines to learn that when he came to Johnstown the common-school system as it has been known to this generation was so unpopular in his new home that there was danger of its complete rejection, while in some of the country districts

surrounding Johnstown it had actually been rejected. Of
all the defenders of the common-school system in Johnstown
at this period Major Potts was certainly the most active, and
the final establishment of the system on a firm foundation
in that town and in neighboring school districts was very
largely the result of his earnest efforts. When the system
was still in danger in Johnstown he was chosen a school
director, and for many years he faithfully and zealously
served his fellow citizens in that humble and thankless position. He was also one of the prime movers in the establishment about 1851 of a select school for girls, which
was held in the building especially erected for the purpose
in the rear of the Presbyterian church and was presided
over by Miss A. L. Elliott and Miss Hannah McCullough,
the latter being succeeded in a year or two by Miss Rebecca Newell. This school was a signal success for many
years. The cause of popular education in Johnstown and
the cause of liberal education as well never had a better
or more efficient friend than Major Potts.

When our old friend came to Johnstown in 1839 his
official position and his natural tastes combined to make
him active in local politics, while his wide acquaintance
with the leading members of his party made him also
to some extent a factor in State politics. He had opinions of his own about men and measures and expressed
them freely. He was long a regular attendant at the county conventions of his party. He was a Tariff Democrat
and a friend of Simon Cameron. He was a ready political writer and liked to take part in newspaper contro-
versies. For a few months in 1846 he was one of the
editors of an independent Democratic paper published in
Johnstown in 1846 and in 1847, called *The Democratic
Courier ;* but a year or two before this, during the inter-
regnum between his retirement from the collector's office
and his entrance upon the active practice of law, he edited for one winter the Democratic organ at Harrisburg,
the *Argus.* In 1847 the *Courier* opposed Governor Shunk's
renomination. It was then edited by T. A. Maguire. The
paper died in that year. In both cases in which Major
Potts assumed editorial duties he was influenced by his

strong partisanship and his thoroughly unselfish devotion to his political friends. With the exceptions which have been noted he never, however, was the recipient of noteworthy political honors. While personally popular with men of all parties his independent and often impulsive methods did not commend him to wide recognition as a party leader.

For several years before the Johnstown flood of May 31, 1889, Judge Potts had lived a quiet and retired life in the comfortable home on Walnut street he had built about 1853, and which was always, especially during the lifetime of Mrs. Potts, one of the most hospitable and inviting of all Johnstown homes. A large garden and many fruit trees occupied much of the judge's attention from spring to fall, and at all seasons his well-stored library served to employ his active brain and to afford subjects of conversation with friends who called to see him. The last conversation I ever held with the judge on the porch of the old-fashioned brick house to which he was so much attached was suggested by his reference to the important part which George Washington had personally taken in the development of Western Pennsylvania. He was an ardent patriot, and the history of his country was as familiar to him as household words, while the achievements of its great men aroused his enthusiasm and excited his pride whenever they were recalled. Western Pennsylvania had a warm place in his affections. He was also a close Bible student and an intelligent adherent of the faith of his fathers. Without pressing his religious views or his biblical knowledge upon others he was always most entertaining when religious or scriptural questions were the subjects of conversation. His knowledge of every subject in which he took an interest was thorough; he could be superficial in nothing which he set out to understand. The early history of Johnstown, its surveys, its metes and bounds, all these were well known to him.

When the flood came on that last day of May, 1889, Judge Potts and his family were overwhelmed by the mighty rush of waters; their home was destroyed in an instant; his oldest daughter, as has already been stated, was lost, although her body was afterwards found; and the judge and his remaining children were swept down toward the now historic stone bridge, where they were rescued. In a day or two the judge and his family found a refuge with friends in Westmoreland county and afterwards with friends in Blair county; thence going before the summer was over to Oil City, where a new home was secured, and where, a few weeks ago, away from the few old friends who had survived the flood, he died.

As my memory carries me back over the fifty years which Judge Potts spent in Johnstown I am impressed by the thought that the town never had a more worthy citizen, never a truer friend, never a more potent force in giving rightful direction to its social and moral development. His influence was always on the right side of every question which affected its welfare, and in his younger days that influence was exerted to the utmost whenever the occasion called for wise leadership. His very presence in the community was in those days an inspiration to the timid, the irresolute, the unfortunate, and the friendless. He was especially the friend of ambitious young men. I can name many successful men who have had Johnstown for their home who owe a great deal of their success in life to the encouragement they received from Judge Potts. His home of refinement and grace was always open to them when they were boys; his books were freely loaned to them; his interest in them never ceased; his praise was never withheld. He was one of the first residents of Johnstown to give to its social currents a literary direction and the desire for the training of colleges and seminaries. But it was in wider directions that his influence for the good of Johnstown was most felt and has been most lasting.

Nearly all the men whose brains and courage and devotion made Johnstown the prosperous and orderly town that it was before the flood have gone to their reward. Now there is a new town among the hills and there are new people in its new homes. It is not surprising to be told that, when Judge Potts visited Johnstown for the last time three months ago, his heart was broken by a flood of memories as crushing as the flood of waters. The old home and the old town gone, old friends gone, himself an old man, what could he do but die and be gathered to his fathers?

JUDGE CYRUS L. PERSHING.

WRITTEN IN 1904 AND PRINTED IN PAMPHLET FORM FOR
PRIVATE CIRCULATION.

AMÓNG the departed great men of Pennsylvania whose
services to the Commonwealth deserve to be gratefully remembered the faithful historian will place Judge Cyrus L.
Pershing, who died on June 29, 1903, at his home in Pottsville, Schuylkill county. Pennsylvanians should be proud
of the fact that this modest but distinguished citizen lived
all his days within the borders of the Keystone State.

The Pershing family is one of the oldest in Western
Pennsylvania. It is of Huguenot origin, Judge Pershing's
great-grandfather, Frederick Pershing, having emigrated to
this country from Alsace, then a part of France, landing at
Baltimore on October 2, 1749. In 1773 the emigrant purchased a tract of 269 acres of land upon the headwaters
of Nine Mile run in what is now Unity township, Westmoreland county, Pennsylvania, and in 1774 he moved his
family from Frederick county, Maryland, to the new home.
With his sons he engaged in farming and he also built
"Pershing's mill." One of his grandsons, Christopher, son
of Christian, was the father of the future judge. Judge
Pershing's mother, Elizabeth Long, was also descended from
a pioneer family in Westmoreland county, her grandfather,
Jacob Long, a Pennsylvania German, having moved from
Lancaster county to Westmoreland county about the begin-
ning of the nineteenth century. Jacob Long's grandfather,
Oswald Long, and his father, Diebold Long, emigrated from
Wurtemberg in 1730.

Cyrus Long Pershing was born at Youngstown, Westmoreland county, on February 3, 1825. He was therefore in
his 79th year at the time of his death. In 1830 his father
moved his family to Johnstown, dying there in 1836. Cyrus was the oldest of three brothers. A good mother was

equal to her responsibilities. That her boys should receive the best education that was possible was her firm determination. They were early sent to "subscription schools." When thirteen years old Cyrus became a clerk in a store in Johnstown. Here he learned from the farmers to speak Pennsylvania Dutch fluently. In 1841, when sixteen years old, he was employed as a clerk at the weighlock of the Pennsylvania Canal at Johnstown. Subsequently he filled other clerical positions in connection with the canal. In all these positions as opportunity would permit he was an industrious student of the educational text books of the day. In 1839 he commenced the study of Latin with Rev. Shadrach Howell Terry, the first pastor of the Presbyterian church at Johnstown, and afterwards he began with Mr. Terry the study of Greek. Mr. Terry died in 1841 and was succeeded by Rev. Samuel Swan. In 1842 Cyrus L. Pershing recited Greek to Mr. Swan that he might be prepared to enter the freshman class of Jefferson College, at Canonsburg, which he entered in November of that year. From this time until June 14, 1848, when he was graduated, he continued his college studies in the winter and his clerical duties in the summer, with the exception of a few months in 1846, when he taught one of the public schools in Johnstown.

During the winter following his graduation Mr. Pershing taught a classical school at Johnstown, which was well attended and was very successful. In 1849, having resolved to study law, he accepted an invitation from Jeremiah S. Black, of Somerset, afterwards the distinguished jurist, to enter his office as a student. In November, 1850, he was admitted to the Somerset bar, and immediately afterwards, on November 26, 1850, he was admitted to the bar of Cambria county. He opened an office in Johnstown for the practice of his profession and at once entered upon a large and profitable practice in the courts of Cambria county. This practice he continued to enjoy as long as he remained a citizen of Johnstown. He also established outside of Cambria county an excellent reputation as a painstaking lawyer who knew the law, and this reputation paved the way for new clients and for honors which soon came

to him. Judge Black was so impressed by the natural
ability of his student and the readiness with which he
mastered legal principles and the details of legal practice
that he offered him a partnership immediately after his
admission to the bar, but this arrangement was not con-
summated because of Judge Black's elevation to the Supreme Bench of Pennsylvania in 1851.

Soon after his admission to the bar Mr. Pershing was
married to Miss Mary Letitia Royer, youngest daughter of
Hon. John Royer, a pioneer iron manufacturer in the Ju-
niata valley and a Whig member of the Legislature from
Huntingdon county and afterwards from Cambria county.
The marriage took place at Mill Creek Furnace on Sep-
tember 23, 1851. Seven children were born to Mr. and Mrs.
Pershing, all of whom, with their mother, are still living.

All lawyers in country towns in the old days were
expected to be politicians, even if they did not have political ambition of their own. Most of them, however, were
ambitious of political preferment. Cyrus L. Pershing was
a politician from boyhood. He knew the history of his
country and of political parties as few other boys knew it.
He early developed literary talent as a writer for the local
newspapers, and what he wrote for publication often relat-
ed to the political issues of the day. He became a member
of a local debating society and soon developed considerable ability as a public speaker. Even before he was admitted to the bar he was in demand as a speaker at
neighborhood meetings of the Democratic party, to which
party he faithfully adhered from the beginning to the end
of his active career. When yet a boy he began to keep
a diary of miscellaneous occurrences and also a scrap-
book of election returns and political events. This habit
of methodically preserving facts which he deemed worthy
of preservation strengthened a naturally retentive memory
and nourished his literary and historical tastes. Running
through his public speeches and addresses while he lived
in Johnstown there was always a historical vein. In 1848,
before his admission to the bar, he was the orator of the
day at a banquet given at Johnstown to the Cambria county
volunteers who had returned from the Mexican war. Few

men who have ever lived in Pennsylvania have known
the history of the State, and especially its political history,
as Cyrus L. Pershing knew it. He was familiar with the
careers of its notable men—politicians, lawyers, clergymen,
college professors, and others, and he had a personal acquaintance with many of them.

After his admission to the bar Mr. Pershing's advance-
ment in the councils and leadership of his party was so
rapid that in 1856 and again in 1858 he was the Democratic candidate for Congress in the district of which
Cambria county formed a part. He was defeated in both
years, as the district was largely Republican in sentiment,
but in each year he greatly reduced the normal anti-
Democratic majority. In the autumn of 1861 he was elected a member of the Legislature from Cambria county, and
he was re-elected in 1862, 1863, 1864, and 1865, serving in
this office for an unusually long and continuous period.
His service in the Legislature ended with the session of
1866. The author of a published sketch of Mr. Pershing
in 1869 says : " During the whole of Mr. Pershing's service
at Harrisburg he was a member of the committee of ways
and means, the judiciary, and other important general and
special committees. At the session of 1863, the only one
in which the Democrats had a majority, Mr. Pershing was
chairman of the committee on federal relations and at the
succeeding session he was the Democratic nominee for
Speaker of the House. He was an acknowledged leader
and enjoyed to a rare degree the confidence and personal
esteem of his fellow members without distinction of party."

It will be observed that Mr. Pershing's services in the
Pennsylvania Legislature covered almost the entire period
of the civil war. He was himself a War Democrat and
believed in the vigorous prosecution of the war. In addition to what is said of Mr. Pershing's legislative career in
the extract above quoted it can be stated as a part of the
history of that great struggle that Governor Curtin was in
the habit of privately consulting with Mr. Pershing as the
Democratic leader in emergencies which were constantly
arising. The Governor could rely on his loyalty, his wisdom, and his influence over his fellow members.

Honors now came to Cyrus L. Pershing in rapid succession. In 1866 he was a delegate from his Congressional district to the National Union Convention which met at Philadelphia in August of that year. In 1868 he was a Presidential elector on the Democratic ticket. In 1869 he was the Democratic candidate for judge of the Supreme Court of Pennsylvania, but was defeated by a small majority. In 1872, owing to divisions in the Democratic party of Schuylkill county, he was asked to become a compromise candidate for president judge of the courts of that county. Mr. Pershing accepted the nomination with some hesitation, remarking to the writer of this sketch that it was always a risk to transplant an old tree. He was then in his 48th year. He had never been in Schuylkill county, and was, of course, a stranger to most of its people, even to many members of the bar who had urged him to accept the nomination. However, he consented to become a candidate and was elected by a large majority for the constitutional term of ten years. In December, 1872, he held his first court at Pottsville and in the spring of 1873 he moved his family to Pottsville. In 1882 he was elected for another term of ten years, and in 1892 for still another term. But failing health prevented him from serving the whole of the third term. He resigned in August, 1899, having presided with great acceptance over the courts of Schuylkill county for twenty-seven consecutive years. From 1899 until his death in 1903 he rested from his labors, but his interest in public affairs and in the welfare of his immediate neighborhood never ceased, and his wonderful memory never failed until he was stricken with his last illness.

In 1875, while presiding over the courts of Schuylkill county, Judge Pershing was nominated for Governor of Pennsylvania by the Democratic State Convention of that year, his opponent being General John F. Hartranft, who had been elected to the Governorship in 1872 and was now a candidate for a second term. Owing to his position on the bench Judge Pershing could not "take the stump." So great, however, was his personal popularity that he was defeated by General Hartranft by a majority of less than 12,000 votes. Outside of Philadelphia he carried the State.

From 1876 to 1878, inclusive, during Judge Pershing's first term as president judge of Schuylkill county, the infamous criminal organization known as the Molly Maguires was completely broken up and many of its members were hung as the result of a series of trials over many of which Judge Pershing presided. This organization had terrorized the anthracite region for several years, and its agents had committed many murders to establish its lawless authority over the mining of anthracite coal. At the risk of his life Judge Pershing did not hesitate to sentence to death the convicted participants in these crimes who were tried before him. From the beginning to the end of these trials he displayed a degree of both physical and moral courage that has never been excelled on the bench. The trials attracted national attention. The law-abiding citizens of Schuylkill county, without respect to party, have never ceased to express their great obligations to Judge Pershing for the courageous part he took in ridding the county of the Mollie Maguire terror. He had been thoroughly tested and found to be pure gold.

Judge Pershing became a member of the First Presbyterian church of Johnstown when still a young man. He became a teacher in its Sunday-school and was afterwards its superintendent for many years. He was a ruling elder in the church when scarcely thirty years old and he continued in the eldership during his residence in Johnstown. After his removal to Pottsville he was chosen to the same office in the Second Presbyterian church of that place, and for many years he taught the Bible class in its Sunday-school. He was a member of the Union Presbyterian Convention which met in Philadelphia in November, 1867, and a member of the General Assembly of the Presbyterian Church which met at Chicago in 1877, at Saratoga in 1884, at Philadelphia in 1888, and at Washington City in 1893.

Judge Pershing was always a loyal friend of his alma mater, Jefferson College, and of the united colleges, Washington and Jefferson. From March, 1865, until June, 1877, when he resigned, he was a trustee of Washington and Jefferson College. At the laying of the corner-stone of the front part of the main college building, on October 21,

1873, Judge Pershing delivered an address. In 1900 the trustees of the college conferred upon him the honorary degree of doctor of laws, an honor that he richly deserved. Judge Pershing died at his home in Pottsville on June 29, 1903, as has already been stated. Never a strong man physically, frail of body but big in intellect, the last few years of his life were a continual struggle against unconquerable disease. The several courts of Schuylkill county at once adjourned when his death became known. On the same day a largely attended meeting of the bench and bar of the county was held at the court-house in Pottsville, at which addresses were delivered and resolutions were adopted which recognized the great services of the deceased jurist and expressed profound appreciation of his lofty private character. It was resolved to attend the funeral in a body. On July 2 the body of Judge Pershing was laid to rest in Mount Laurel cemetery, in Pottsville, in sight of the beautiful home on the hillside in which he had lived with his wife and children for thirty years.

The services at the house and at the grave were rendered particularly impressive by the presence of Rev. Dr. Benjamin L. Agnew, the secretary of the board of ministerial relief of the Presbyterian Church. Dr. Agnew was for ten years the pastor of the First Presbyterian church of Johnstown, and during the whole of this period Judge Pershing was one of his elders and one of his most intimate friends. Dr. Agnew and Judge Pershing were born in adjoining counties—Dr. Agnew in Armstrong county and Judge Pershing in Westmoreland county.

At the meeting of the bench and bar of Schuylkill county on the day of Judge Pershing's death President Judge Bechtel, the chairman, said: "No one ever faced his duty more conscientiously than Judge Pershing. He came here to preside over a court which had the distinction of having a bar membership second to none in the great State of Pennsylvania. He was called upon at that time to dispose of most intricate civil, equitable, and other legal questions. He lived through it all and performed his duties faithfully, sincerely, and earnestly. His action in his official capacity brought honor and greatness to him. His decisions were quoted as authority throughout the State by such eminent jurists as Judge Elwell and others, and were considered akin to decisions of the Supreme Court." On the day of his death the newspapers of Pottsville referred to the character and services of Judge Pershing in most kindly terms. The *Chronicle* said : " In the death of Hon. Cyrus L. Pershing Schuylkill county loses one of its most eminent and honored citizens and the State a jurist whose record was second to none. Judge Pershing came to Schuylkill county untried upon the bench. He soon, however, demonstrated the wisdom of his selection, for no man ever did more to raise the standard of the bench of Schuylkill county than he. His private life was spotless, his career upon the bench above criticism, and when he voluntarily retired from public life he carried with him the highest esteem and sincere love of the entire county which he had so zealously and ably served." The *Republican* said : " Pottsville and Schuylkill county have lost a distinguished citizen by the death of Judge Cyrus L. Pershing. Judge Pershing was a man of large mental capacity, powerful will, sterling character, and the strictest integrity. His private life, in the church and in the precincts of the home circle, was a model one. Judge Pershing was one of the representative men of Pottsville, one whose memory is a precious heritage."

Cyrus L. Pershing was a thoroughly equipped lawyer, a wise and just judge, a politician who sought the public welfare and a man of wide influence in the promotion of many good works. But the world can not know, as his intimate friends knew, and especially as his old friends knew, how hard, how very hard, was the struggle that he was compelled to make to fit himself for the duties that fell to his lot. From a child he was handicapped by weak eyesight, and in his ambition to obtain a liberal education he had no assistance, but he never faltered in that ambition from the time he recited his first Latin lesson, and he literally paid his own way through a college course. All his subsequent success was due to the same courageous spirit and to his remarkable industry. He was no idler, no trifler with precious time. The work that was given him to do he did with all his might. All his life he was a student, not only of books but also of men and events. Withal he was sociable, genial, and kind-hearted. His wonderful memory of historical events and his recollections of public men, joined to a vein of the keenest humor and to a ready wit that no bodily affliction ever suppressed, made him a delightful companion for old and young. And yet, looking back upon his long and useful and honorable life, no trait in his character appeals to us with so much force as the brave fight he made against mighty odds to secure a liberal education and a mastery of his profession. He was pre-eminently a man of courage. He conquered difficulties that would have appalled most men and he feared no man.

COLONEL JACOB M. CAMPBELL.

AN EDITORIAL IN THE JOHNSTOWN TRIBUNE OF FRIDAY,.
AUGUST 25, 1865, WITH ADDENDA.

THE importance of the pending political campaign in
this State, and the enthusiasm everywhere created among
loyal men by the nomination of two distinguished soldiers
for the only offices to be filled this year on the State ticket,.
naturally call for more than a brief reference to the antecedents and characteristics of our Republican standard-bearers.
In another place we give such information as we possess
concerning the civic and military record of Major General
Hartranft, the candidate for auditor general, and in this
article we propose to tell what we know about our friend
and fellow-citizen, Colonel Campbell, the nominee for surveyor general.

Jacob Miller Campbell is a native of that old Whig
stronghold, Somerset county, where he was born forty-four
years ago in Allegheny township on November 20, 1821.
He was the son of John and Mary (Weyand) Campbell.
When a mere youth his parents removed to Allegheny City,
where he went to school until 1835. In that year, being
fourteen years old, he became an apprentice in the office
of the *Somerset Whig*, a Democratic newspaper, in which he
remained until he had mastered as much of the printing
business as could be learned in a country office of that· day.
In 1840 he left Somerset and worked for some time "at
case" in the office of the *Literary Examiner*, a monthly
magazine of considerable merit, published in Pittsburgh.
From here our "jour printer" found his way to New Orleans and to another printing office. But his active nature
was not satisfied. The steamboat trade on the lower Missis-
sippi presented in 1840, as does the oil business in 1865,
tempting inducements to enterprising spirits who care less
for hard knocks than for the substantial benefits which they

sometimes produce. Laying down his composing stick the boy of nineteen became a steamboatman, and for several subsequent years he filled successively the positions of clerk, mate, and part owner of a steamboat, always, however, making Pennsylvania his home, which he frequently visited. In 1847 the iron business of our State attracted his attention and he embarked in it at Brady's Bend, working as a roller in a rolling mill. In the same year he married. In 1851 he followed the course of empire to California but did not long remain there, and in 1853 we find him in Johnstown assisting in the construction of our mammoth rolling mill. With this splendid enterprise he remained connected up to the breaking out of the war, holding all the time an important and responsible position.

In April, 1861, Fort Sumter was fired upon and the call appeared for volunteers to "rally round the flag." At that time Mr. Campbell was first lieutenant of a volunteer company in Johnstown, and his company at once tendered its services to the Governor, who promptly accepted them. It was the first company to enter Camp Curtin. Upon the organization of the Third Regiment of Pennsylvania Volunteers for three months' service this company became known as Company G. Lieutenant Campbell was appointed quartermaster of the regiment, a position which he filled with great acceptance until the regiment was discharged. On the 28th of July he was mustered out of service, and on the 30th he was authorized to recruit a regiment for three years' service. In due time the regiment was completed and he was commissioned its colonel, the companies composing it having been largely recruited through his individual efforts. Eight of the ten companies were recruited in Cambria and Somerset counties and two in Lehigh and Northampton counties. The regiment when mustered into service was designated the Fifty-fourth.

For two years this regiment performed the arduous duty of guarding sixty miles of the Baltimore and Ohio Railroad, and while thus engaged it protected the Maryland and Pennsylvania border from Rebel invasion and from guerrilla outrages. It is a fact that may not be generally known to Pennsylvanians that to the Fifty-fourth Regiment they

owe much of the security they enjoyed in their persons and
property during 1862 and 1863, the two most critical years
of the war. The position of the Fifty-fourth was at all
times an exceedingly dangerous one, requiring the exercise
of the utmost vigilance and the soundest discretion. During its guardianship of the railroad it was frequently engaged in skirmishes with the enemy, and upon more than
one occasion it gave timely and valuable information of
his movements and designs. In addition to his ordinary
duties as commander of the regiment Colonel Campbell was
almost daily called upon to decide disputes between the
Rebels and Unionists residing along the line of the railroad, and it is no exaggeration to say that in no instance
was justice cheated or rascality rewarded. It is not an as-
sertion merely, but the testimony of all who are cognizant
of the facts, that the commander of the Fifty-fourth manifested on all occasions the possession of judicial qualities
of a high order. Of his purely executive ability the successful and always satisfactory manner in which the regiment guarded those sixty miles of railroad in hostile territory is the only proof that we need to cite. We had almost
omitted to mention that from March, 1863, until March,
1864, Colonel Campbell was in command of the Fourth
Brigade, First Division, Eighth Army Corps, in which was
included his own regiment.

Early in 1864 General Sigel took command of the Department of West Virginia and moved with all his availa-
ble troops to Martinsburg, preparatory to a movement up
the Shenandoah valley. In a reorganization of the troops
which then took place Colonel Campbell, at his own request,
returned to the command of his regiment. At the battle
of New Market, on May 15, 1864, the regiment suffered severely. It occupied the extreme left of the line and was
the last to leave the field.

Under General Hunter the Fifty-fourth Regiment took a
prominent part in the battle of Piedmont, on June 5, 1864,
again occupying the left of the line, and this time flanking
the enemy's right and attacking him in the rear. After the
battle Colonel Campbell was assigned to the command of a
brigade and as a special favor his own regiment was trans-

ferred to it, that it might remain under its old commander. The brigade suffered heavily in an attack on the Rebel entrenchments at Lynchburg and covered the retreat of the army when the attack failed. On July 24 the brigade participated in the battle of Winchester and upon the fall of Colonel Mulligan Colonel Campbell took command of his division. He continued in command until its consolidation into a brigade, consequent upon its many losses in killed and wounded, and he afterwards commanded the brigade. After General Sheridan came to the head of the department the brigade participated in the engagements in the Shenandoah valley under that renowned commander. Colonel Campbell was mustered out of service nearly two months after the expiration of his three years' term of enlistment. His total period of service, including the three months' campaign, covered nearly three and a half years.

Colonel Campbell's early record as a politician will bear examination. Reared in the school of Jacksonian Democracy he voted in 1844 for Polk and Dallas. In 1848, however, he abandoned the party which he had become convinced was the champion of slavery extension, and the foe to Pennsylvania's best interests, and voted for the Free Soil candidates, Van Buren and Adams. His residence in the South had shown him the evils of slavery and he therefore gave his vote against the party which sought its extension. In 1852 he voted again for the Free Soil nominees, Hale and Julian. In 1856 he was the delegate from Cambria county to the Fremont Convention, which met at Musical Fund Hall in Philadelphia. During that year he took an active part in advocating Republican principles in his own county, and at once took rank with the people of the county as a politician of fairness, ability, and zeal. His influence in county politics continued to be felt during the succeeding years. In 1859 he was the choice of the Republicans of Cambria county for the Senatorial nomination in the district composed of Cambria, Blair, and Clearfield counties, and a little more than a month ago he was again unanimously selected as the choice of the Union party of his county for Senator from the district composed of Cambria, Indiana, and Jefferson counties. That he was not nominated on either occasion by the district conference was not owing to a want of appreciation of his worth and services, but was due to the supposed superior claims of the county which was honored with the nominee. Such is the private and public record of our candidate for surveyor general.

Colonel Campbell is a shrewd business man, a public spirited citizen, a good worker, and an honest man. Without having enjoyed the advantages of a liberal education he is, nevertheless, one of the best read men in the State. He is a clear thinker and remarkably cool and cautious in judgment. In a long acquaintance we have rarely known him to err in his estimate of public men or in the wisdom of public measures. He is a man of marked sagacity. His social characteristics are of that class which never fails to create the warmest friendships and to command the respect of all. That he is worthy of the office for which he has been nominated is conceded by those who know the man. That he and his gallant colleague, General Hartranft, will be elected by overwhelming majorities is a foregone conclusion.

The foregoing sketch of Colonel Campbell was written when he was the Republican candidate for surveyor general in 1865. He was elected to that office for the term of three years on the ticket with General Hartranft for auditor general. In 1868 both gentlemen were re-elected to the same offices, each serving another term of three years. In 1876 Colonel Campbell was elected a Republican Representative to the 45th Congress from the 17th district of Pennsylvania, composed of the counties of Bedford, Blair, Cambria, and Somerset, receiving a majority of 520 votes over John Reilly, his Democratic opponent. In 1878 he was a candidate for re-election but was defeated by A. H. Coffroth by a majority of 305. In 1880 he was elected to the 47th Congress by a majority of 1,436 over A. H. Coffroth, and in 1882 he was elected to the 48th Congress by a majority of 551 over the same opponent. He was elected to the 49th Congress by a majority of 3,564 over Americus Enfield. It will be seen that Colonel Campbell represented his district in Congress for the exceptionally long period of eight years, a fact which forcibly testifies to his popularity and ability.

An incident in the life of Colonel Campbell, illustrating his patriotism, should not go unrecorded. When in the service of Wood, Morrell & Co. he worked under a tonnage contract for several years, employing his own helpers. This contract was profitable. When the civil war came and it was necessary for Pennsylvania to borrow a large sum of money to make preparation to assist the Government at Washington in resisting rebellion Colonel Campbell promptly subscribed $30,000 to the State loan, which represented virtually all his savings. At the time this subscription was made the risk of payment of both interest and principal was very great, as all who passed through those trying times will well remember. More than one friend of Colonel Campbell said that he would never see his money again.

On April 28, 1847, Colonel Campbell was married to Mary Rankin Campbell (no relative) at Brady's Bend. He died at Johnstown on September 27, 1888, aged nearly 67 years. His wife and several children survived him.

ALEXANDER CHESTERFIELD MULLIN.

WRITTEN IN NOVEMBER, 1878, AND PRINTED IN PAMPHLET
FORM FOR PRIVATE CIRCULATION.

DIED, at his residence, No. 1735 Oxford street, Philadelphia, on Friday, November 22, 1878, Alexander Chesterfield Mullin, aged 48 years, 2 months, and 3 days.

Mr. Mullin was born on the 19th day of September, 1830, in the town of Bedford, Pennsylvania, in the historic structure known then and now as the Old Fort. His parents were George and Catharine Mullin, the father a native of Cumberland county, Pennsylvania, and the mother, whose maiden name was Hammer, a native of Frederick county, Maryland. George Mullin was for many years a prominent citizen of Bedford county. In the fall of 1836, at the close of his second term as sheriff, he removed his family to the Mansion Farm, on the Wheeling turnpike, six miles west of Bedford, which he had purchased in 1818. Here his son Alexander lived, a farmer's boy, until he went from the parental roof, when little more than seventeen years old. He was the youngest of seven brothers. Three of the brothers were in the Union army. Both the grandfathers of this family served in the Revolutionary war.

While living in Bedford Alexander attended the Bedford Academy. After the family removed to the farm, in 1836, it was the good fortune of Alexander to be sent to several excellent subscription schools in the neighborhood. Alexander's mathematical studies extended to trigonometry and other branches connected with surveying. Attending school in both summer and winter, and being favored with good teachers, he made rapid progress. He also wrote verses, learned to sketch, and joined a country debating society. When a little more than seventeen years old he taught school for two months in Londonderry valley.

In May, 1848, Alexander left home to become a clerk in

the store of his bachelor uncle, David Hammer, at Hollidaysburg, Blair county. It may be incidentally mentioned here that Joseph Hammer, another uncle, was for several years, from about 1849 to 1852, the landlord of Bennett's Hotel, at Johnstown, for whom and for his excellent family the old citizens of the town cherish most pleasant recollections. Alexander's engagement with his uncle did not, however, long continue, for, after four months' experience in his store, and when just eighteen years old, we find him, in September, taking charge of the lumber interests of Robert Lytle at Wilmore, in Cambria county, who also kept a store at the same place, in which William C. Barbour was a clerk. Robert Lytle was a resident of Hollidaysburg. In April, 1849, Alexander was offered by George Murray a clerkship in his store at Summerhill, in Cambria county, which offer was accepted, and in the latter part of the month he entered upon his new duties. The situation proved to be a pleasant one, and for three years it was filled by Alexander with great satisfaction to his employer.

At Summerhill Alexander continued in his leisure hours the study of mathematics and Latin, being greatly aided by an educated Irish shoemaker named George G. Higgins, who had spent many years of his life on the ocean. Having thus obtained a part of that additional education he had longed for when he left home, and having acquired considerable business experience, he resolved to study law, and accordingly, in November, 1851, he entered his name as a student with Edward Hutchinson, Jr., a prominent member of the Ebensburg bar. He began immediately the usual course of legal studies, and from this time on until May, 1852, while still remaining at Summerhill, his time was about equally divided between these studies and the settlement of Mr. Murray's business, which had for a number of years been very extensive. At the time last named above Alexander, then familiarly known as "Aleck," but whom I shall hereafter call Mr. Mullin, went to Ebensburg, with the double purpose of prosecuting his legal studies under the direction of Mr. Hutchinson and acting as clerk to the prothonotary of the county, Robert L. Johnston, who had solicited his assistance in rearranging all the records of the office since the organization of the county in 1807. Mr. Mullin's skill as an accountant and bookkeeper and the elegance and neatness of his penmanship had by this time become generally known throughout Cambria county, and Mr. Johnston's choice of him as an assistant was therefore wisely made and proved to be very popular. At that day the duties of the prothonotary's office embraced the recording of deeds and also the registering of wills. Mr. Mullin remained with Mr. Johnston until the close of the latter's term of office in the fall of 1854, when they entered into partnership, the style of the firm being Johnston & Mullin. This partnership continued for five years.

On the 27th day of October, 1852, Mr. Mullin was married at Williamsburg by Rev. John Thrush to Miss Emma Matilda Kennedy, a native of Perry county, Pennsylvania, but at the time a resident of Rockdale, Blair county.

In August, 1853, the want of a Whig newspaper at Ebensburg having long been felt, Mr. Mullin and a friend of about his own age, named Charles Albright, since well known to fame as a lawyer, soldier, and politician, but then a student in the law office of Mr. Johnston, were induced, under the firm name of Mullin & Albright, to establish *The Alleghanian*. The paper was a weekly, of six columns, well printed, and from the first was well edited. Coming into existence during a heated canvass for a seat in the State Senate from the district composed of Cambria, Blair, and Huntingdon counties *The Alleghanian* took decided ground against the candidacy of Alexander M. White, of Cambria county, who had secured the nomination by the Whig senatorial conference. So vigorous was its opposition that Mr. White was defeated by the Democratic nominee, John Creswell, Jr., of Hollidaysburg, although the district, by conviction, belonged to the Whigs. The bitterness of the contest was carried into the courts, where legal proceedings were inaugurated, but nothing of moment came of them. The course of *The Alleghanian* in this matter was generally justified by the leading Whigs of the district. The connection of Mullin & Albright with the paper was continued until 1854, when they were succeeded in its publication by J. R. Durburrow and he soon afterwards by John M. Bowman.

At December term, 1853, of the Cambria county courts Mr. Mullin was admitted to the bar, on motion of Michael Dan Magehan, with whom had been associated Henry D. Foster and James Potts on the committee of examination. Hon. George Taylor, president judge, and Hon. Evan Roberts and Hon. Harrison Kinkead, associates, were on the bench. The bar of Cambria county in 1853 was one of great native and reflected ability. Of the resident members I can remember Edward Hutchinson, Jr., Robert L. Johnston, Charles H. Heyer, John S. Rhey, Michael Dan Magehan, Joseph McDonald, Michael Hasson, John Fenlon, Cyrus L. Pershing, James Potts, Abram Kopelin, Theophilus L. Heyer, Moses Canan, William Kittell, Samuel C. Wingard, Charles W. Wingard, George M. Reade, John F. Barnes, and Charles D. Murray—not all good lawyers, it is true, but as a body they formed the best bar the county could ever boast. Of visiting lawyers from neighboring counties there were John G. Miles and John Scott, of Huntingdon; S. S. Blair and David H. Hofius, of Blair; Thomas White, of Indiana; and Henry D. Foster, Edgar Cowan, and Wm. A. Stokes, of Westmoreland. These men were all able lawyers. The bench was more than respectable. Judge Taylor was one of the ablest judges in the State and the associates were men of high social standing and good judgment. Mr. Mullin came to the bar under most favorable circumstances.

Mr. Mullin had a strong inclination to engage in the excitements and to enjoy some of the rewards of political life. Thus we find him in 1855 the candidate of the new American party for treasurer of Cambria county, but he was beaten, in a contest hopeless from the beginning, by Charles D. Murray, Democrat. In 1856 he was the Union Republican candidate for the State Senate in the Cambria, Blair, and Huntingdon district, but was defeated by John Creswell, Jr., of Blair, although running ahead of his ticket in his own county. In 1857 he was selected by the unanimous vote of the judges of the Cambria, Blair, and Huntingdon judicial district as a member of the State board of revenue revision. In this position he so skillfully protected the interests of his constituents that a proposition to increase their taxes, made by Hendrick B. Wright, a member of the board, and supported by others, was so amended as to effect an actual lowering of them. In 1859 he re-established *The Alleghanian,* the publication of which had been discontinued some time previously, and at once made it a vigorous exponent of Republican principles. He owned the paper and was its editor, but its publication was intrusted to two young men whose firm name was Bolsinger & Hutchinson. In a brief time this firm was dissolved, and J. Todd Hutchinson continued the publication of the paper, with Mr. Mullin as owner and editor. Mr. Mullin's connection with *The Alleghanian* continued until 1861, when he sold it to A. A. Barker, who retained Mr. Hutchinson as publisher.

In the fall of 1860 Mr. Mullin was chosen a Representative from Cambria county to the Pennsylvania Legislature. The contest in which he was the successful candidate was a quadrangular one—George Nelson Smith representing the Douglas Democrats, Michael Dan Magehan the Breckinridge Democrats, James Potts the advocates of a new county, and Mr. Mullin the Union Republicans. The plurality of Mr. Mullin over his highest opponent, Major Smith, was a little less than 300.

The Legislature met on the 1st of January, 1861, and Mr. Mullin was present. Upon the organization of the House he was assigned to the committee on ways and means and to the committee on new counties and county seats. The assignment to the first of these committees would have conveyed a very high compliment under ordinary legislative circumstances, but a contingency soon to happen, and dreaded when the session opened, made the position one of great responsibility and importance. We were drifting into a war with the Southern States, and the attitude which Pennsylvania should take in the struggle, and the strength and resolution with which she should maintain that attitude, largely depended upon the ways and means committee of the House of Representatives. During the regular session, and the special session which soon followed it, Mr. Mullin supported every measure of legislation that was designed to sustain the power of the Federal Government, including the bill to borrow money and the bill to organize and equip the Pennsylvania Reserve Corps. He had no patience with the Peace Conference or with any other temporizing expedient.

As a legislator Mr. Mullin paid strict attention to the interests of his constituents. Of the bills which were considered during the session eighteen were passed through his instrumentality. Some of the bills that were introduced and passed by Mr. Mullin were of considerable local importance. One of these gave greatly needed relief to the Cambria Iron Company and enabled the lessees, Messrs. Wood, Morrell & Co., to continue the works in operation during many months which would otherwise have been lost to them and their workmen.

After the adjournment of the Legislature in the spring of 1861 Mr. Mullin continued the practice of his profession until September, 1862, when he was appointed private secretary to Governor Curtin. He never again regularly practiced his profession. Retaining his home at Ebensburg he immediately assumed at Harrisburg the most arduous and responsible duties of his life. A great war was in progress and the State of Pennsylvania took no insignificant part in the contest. The duties of the Governor were increased many fold, and to aid him in the performance of his difficult task the service of the best executive and administrative talent of the State was called into requisition. The choice of a private secretary could not have been more happily made than in the selection of Mr. Mullin. He remained with the Governor until after the close of the war, during part of the time assisting to discharge the duties of master of transportation in addition to those of private secretary.

It is a pleasure to me to record here an incident which illustrates the friendly personal relations which have always in a large degree existed between leading members of opposing political parties in Cambria county. Cyrus L. Pershing represented Cambria county in the lower branch of the Legislature in 1862 and was consulted by Governor Curtin concerning the appointment of Mr. Mullin as private secretary. Mr. Pershing assured the Governor that he could find no person better adapted to the duties of the position than Mr. Mullin and that he could implicitly rely upon his fidelity.

Soon after peace had come Mr. Mullin decided to re-
linquish the onerous duties at Harrisburg which had gradually affected his health and accordingly resigned the office
of private secretary to the Governor on the 1st of May,
1865, to embark in business in Philadelphia. He afterwards looked upon the decision to go to Philadelphia as a
mistake and regretted bitterly that he did not return to
the practice of law among his old friends at Ebensburg.
But the times were abnormal and the wild wave of speculation swept the best and coolest men before it. Mr. Mullin
had, while at Harrisburg, made some small investments in
the stocks of the day which proved to be profitable, and
this experience, joined to the unsatisfactory condition of his
health, was the impelling motive which led him to yield
to the liberal offers of some of his friends that he should
go to Philadelphia to exercise a general supervision over
several speculative enterprises in which they were interested. He went, but the enterprises of his friends, as well as
some investments of his own, met with disaster.

In May, 1866, the position of chief clerk of the State
Department at Harrisburg became vacant and Mr. Mullin
was appointed to the vacancy. His predecessor, William W.
Hays, had been promoted to be Deputy Secretary of the
Commonwealth, but the health of this gentleman was so
seriously impaired that many of the duties of his new office
fell to the lot of Mr. Mullin, in addition to the laborious
exactions of the chief clerkship. The preparation of par-
dons was included in Mr. Mullin's extraordinary duties.
All the correspondence of the State Department he either
directed or performed. The pamphlet laws of 1866, the
most voluminous ever published, he edited.

In the latter part of September, 1866, Mr. Mullin was
appointed by President Johnson collector of internal revenue
for the seventeenth district of Pennsylvania, with his office
at Ebensburg, relieving Samuel J. Royer, of Johnstown, and
at once entered upon his duties. Political feeling had been
deeply stirred by the antagonism existing between the President and the party which had elected him, and to the
impatience of the Republicans with the President's alleged
arbitrary exercise of power in removing faithful Republican

officials may mainly be attributed the failure of the Senate in March following to confirm Mr. Mullin's appointment. This rejection of Mr. Mullin's appointment was an unfortunate event in his life. Soon after his rejection he closed his accounts as collector and paid over to the deputy collector of the district the money remaining in his hands.

After the termination of the episode which has just been described Mr. Mullin was about to resume the practice of law when he was offered and accepted the position of cashier of the Dime Savings Institution of Ashland, Schuylkill county, which had just been chartered. Of this bank Peter F. Collins, of Ebensburg, was president. The name of the bank was changed a year or two later to the Ashland Savings Bank. Mr. Mullin sold his house in Ebensburg and removed his family to Ashland in the fall of 1867. In 1870 he became president of the bank, Mr. Collins retiring, and he remained in this position until the spring of 1875, when the bank failed through the pressure of many adverse circumstances, most of which had their origin in the Jay Cooke panic of 1873. The severity of the crisis which caused Mr. Mullin to close his bank is seen in the fact that most of the neighboring banks afterwards passed out of existence.

Toward the latter part of 1875 Mr. Mullin, having no promising future before him in Ashland, began to think of removing to Philadelphia. In March, 1876, after residing eight years and a half in Ashland, he was appointed secretary of the Pennsylvania Board of Centennial Managers, of which Morton McMichael was chairman and Andrew G. Curtin, Asa Packer, Daniel J. Morrell, John H. Shoenberger, George Scott, and Foster W. Mitchell were associates. Mr. Mullin at once removed his family to Philadelphia. He was laboriously engaged in the performance of his new duties until the spring of 1878, when the functions of the board virtually terminated with the presentation to the Pennsylvania Legislature by the Governor of Mr. Mullin's admirable report, printed in two handsome octavo volumes, detailing the work of the board and the part taken by Pennsylvania in connection with the Centennial Exhibition.

I now take up some incidents in the life of Mr. Mullin of a more private character than those already mentioned.

He had a fondness for military life. At Summerhill, about September, 1849, when only nineteen years old, he assisted in forming the Quitman Guards, a volunteer company, of which William M. Ott, who had been in the Mexican war, was elected captain. The company was organized by Major John Linton, of Johnstown, brigade inspector. Mr. Mullin was at first a private in the company but soon rose to be second lieutenant and then first lieutenant. He was offered the captaincy in 1852, which he was obliged to decline, as he was about to leave Summerhill for Ebensburg. William C. Barbour became captain of the company until it was disbanded a few years afterwards. The Quitman Guards always celebrated the national anniversaries with great spirit. I am reminded by Judge Pershing that Lieutenant Mullin delivered an oration on a 4th of July which the Guards assisted to celebrate and that it was published in one or more of the county newspapers. Many members of the Guards entered the Union army and rendered their country good service.

Mr. Mullin possessed decided literary tastes and literary talent of a high order. When fourteen years old he wrote Whig campaign songs and negro melodies which are yet remembered in Bedford county. Throughout his whole life he wrote verses—humorous, satirical, lyrical, and elegiac.

While at Ebensburg Mr. Mullin not only assisted in establishing *The Alleghanian*, which he edited with true journalistic insight for several years, but he also attached himself to a good literary society of which he long continued an active member and was frequently its presiding officer. The society maintained a literary paper, and of this Mr. Mullin was at various times the editor. In the pamphlet laws of 1866 and in his masterly Centennial report the tact and judgment of the born editor are plainly seen. He always wrote gracefully and rapidly, knew a good word from a bad one, and could quit when he was done. Mr. Mullin was an ardent lover of the English classics. Shakespeare and Dickens were his favorite authors, and he knew them well. He was well versed in the history of his country and was familiar with the careers of its leading men.

When a boy Mr. Mullin evinced a strong passion for

sketching and painting, but this taste was but slightly gratified until years afterwards, when he painted in oil several pictures of much merit. I can not praise too highly his artistic achievements in ornamental penmanship. He was one of the best penmen who ever resided in Cambria county, and in purely ornamental work with the pen he had few, if any, superiors in the State.

Mr. Mullin was a public-spirited citizen of Ebensburg while he lived there. At various times he served as a member of its school board and town council. In 1857 he was largely instrumental in creating the Cambria County Mutual Fire Insurance Company, of which he was secretary and treasurer. He also rendered valuable assistance in securing in July, 1862, the completion of the Ebensburg Branch of the Pennsylvania Railroad, the construction of which was commenced about 1858. This assistance he was enabled to give while a member of the Legislature in 1861.

Of Mr. Mullin's legal abilities and legal attainments it is enough to say that he won deserved praise from the bench and the bar for the accuracy and neatness of all legal instruments which emanated from his hand. So well established was his reputation as a well-read lawyer, and as an accomplished expert in the preparation of legal documents, that in 1866 all the members of the bar of the twenty-fourth judicial district, embracing Cambria, Blair, and Huntingdon counties, signed a recommendation that he be appointed reporter of the decisions of the Supreme Court of Pennsylvania. The appointment, however, went to another.

The social qualities of Mr. Mullin were of a very high order and he was greatly favored with rare opportunities for their development. When he went to Ebensburg, in addition to making acquaintance with the wit and learning of the bar, the medical fraternity was composed of Dr. William A. Smith, Dr. David W. Lewis, and Dr. William Lemon. Ezekiel Hughes, Edward Shoemaker, and Johnston Moore were leading business men. Major John Thompson kept the leading hotel of the place and his estimable family was then intact. Then there were the Noons, the Rheys, the Collinses, the McDonalds, and many other excellent families, embracing talented men and accomplished women.

SAMUEL BELL McCORMICK.

COMMUNICATED TO THE JOHNSTOWN TRIBUNE IN APRIL,
1901, DURING MR. McCORMICK'S LIFETIME.

RECENT references in the columns of the *Tribune* to the
old-time schools and school teachers of Johnstown and its
vicinity prompt me to compile from data in my possession
the leading facts in the career of Samuel Bell McCormick,
a noted teacher of fifty years ago in Johnstown.

S. B. McCormick, as he has always written his name,
was born on a farm a short distance south of what is now
Larimer Station, on the Pennsylvania Railroad, in Westmoreland county, on June 18, 1817. His father, Andrew
McCormick, was a native of the north of Ireland and came
to this country with his father, John McCormick, and the
remainder of the family in 1790, when he was six years
old. The McCormicks came directly from Ireland to Larimer with a large colony of Scotch-Irish, the Griers, the Bax-
ters, the Boyds, the Irwins, and others. They built a church
on Matthew Osborn's land, and there are yet in the churchyard forty tombstones of McCormicks, although the church
was torn down long ago. S. B. McCormick's mother, whose
maiden name was Ann Campbell, the daughter of James
Campbell, at one time a rich and prosperous Philadelphia
merchant, was born in Philadelphia in 1786. The Campbells were also Scotch-Irish, James Campbell coming from
the north of Ireland to this country before the Revolution.
In course of time James Campbell, with his family, also
moved to Western Pennsylvania, the Campbells finally set-
tling in the Redstone settlement on the Monongahela river.
We give these details partly to illustrate the prominence of
the Scotch-Irish element in the early settlement of Western
Pennsylvania.

Andrew McCormick became the owner of a piece of land
near Larimer Station. From the Larimer farm Mr. Mc-

Cormick's father moved to Murrysville, where the family resided for seven years. Thence Andrew McCormick moved to Warsaw, in Jefferson county, in 1835, and died there. S. B. McCormick was almost wholly self-educated. He was never a student at either a college or an academy. Gifted with an acute intellect, ambitious, and studious, he was not satisfied with the limited opportunities afforded by the subscription schools of his day and aspired to better things. He studied geometry with his oldest brother, Latin with a preacher named Marshall and with the Reverend W. W. Woodend, Greek with Thomas B. Keenan, and astronomy without any assistance except that which he first obtained from a "geography of the heavens." When Mr. McCormick was a young man land surveying was one of the learned professions; a surveyor of farms and roads was a person of consequence; so S. B. McCormick studied surveying with an expert surveyor in Brookville, Jefferson county, after the family had removed to that county. But prior to going to Jefferson county Mr. McCormick began in Westmoreland county his life work as a teacher.

S. B. McCormick's father was an Associate Reformed Presbyterian, and having many religious books the son was posted in Bible history and theological questions. For a time, soon after he had commenced teaching, he was a member of Dr. David Kirkpatrick's Bible class at Poke Run Presbyterian church.

In 1840 Mr. McCormick taught school near New Alexandria, Westmoreland county. One of his pupils was the present Judge A. D. McConnell, of Greensburg, who learned his A B C's at Mr. McCormick's knee. About 1844 Mr. McCormick began the study of law with Hon. Joseph H. Kuhns, of Greensburg, at one time a Whig member of Congress, and was admitted to the Westmoreland bar on September 3, 1846. On September 5, 1846, he was married to Eliza Kemp and moved to Ligonier, where he taught school, practiced law, and started a newspaper. In 1852, with his wife and two children, he moved to Johnstown and began his career as a Cambria county teacher. From that time until his removal to California in 1874 he taught school at Johnstown and Millville, except during a period of five years when he served as superintendent of common schools for Cambria county. Mr. McCormick lives at Oakdale, Stanislaus county, California, where for many years he was a local magistrate, with the honorary title of judge. He taught school for two years at Oakdale. His son, Winfield Scott McCormick, had preceded him to Oakdale.

Mr. McCormick's long career as a teacher in Johnstown was a most honorable one. Thoroughly understanding all the branches of study that were embraced in the sensible common-school course of those days he was very successful in leading his classes up the hill of science and in developing in hundreds of boys and girls who are now getting to be old men and women the ambition to do their best in the school-room and in the wider spheres which they were soon to enter. For several years he was superintendent of the Johnstown schools. He was also principal of the Millville schools for three or four years. He had a special liking for astronomy and often lectured upon this subject.

In November, 1852, soon after his removal from Ligonier to Johnstown, and while teaching at the head of Main street, Mr. McCormick undertook the publication of a weekly Whig newspaper, *The Cambrian*, which he continued until about the close of the political campaign in the fall of 1853, when its publication was discontinued. The printing materials were owned by some of the leading Whigs of the town. The *Cambria Tribune* was established in December, 1853, immediately after Mr. McCormick's retirement. With a decided literary bent and possessed of considerable skill as a newspaper controversialist Mr. McCormick could not successfully teach school and edit a newspaper, either at Ligonier or Johnstown, nor could anybody.

The common school system of Pennsylvania was not fully developed until 1854, on May 8 of which year an act of the General Assembly was approved by Governor William Bigler which established the office of county superintendent. The act took effect the same year. Robert L. Johnston was the first superintendent for Cambria county and Mr. McCormick was the second. I copy below from the official record a list of the persons who have held this office in Cambria county from 1854 to the present time.

Robert L. Johnston, elected; commissioned July 5, 1854; resigned in 1855; salary per annum, $400. S. B. McCormick, appointed; commissioned October 6, 1855; salary, $400. S. B. McCormick, elected for three years; commissioned June 3, 1857; salary, $800. Thomas A. Maguire, elected; commissioned July 17, 1860; salary, $800. James M. Swank, appointed; commissioned February 7, 1861; resigned in November, 1861; salary, $800. Wm. A. Scott, appointed; commissioned January 4, 1862; salary, $800; resigned to enter the Union army; killed at Fredericksburg. Henry Ely, appointed; commissioned August 13, 1862; salary, $800. J. Frank Condon, elected; commissioned June 1, 1863; salary, $800; J. Frank Condon, re-elected; commissioned June 4, 1866; salary, $1,000; resigned in 1867. T. J. Chapman, appointed; commissioned October 1, 1867. T. J. Chapman, elected; commissioned June 4, 1869; salary, $1,000. T. J. Chapman, re-elected; commissioned June 6, 1872; salary, $1,000. Hartman Berg, elected; commissioned June 7, 1875; salary, $1,000; re-elected; commissioned June, 1878. L. Strayer, elected; commissioned June, 1881; salary fixed by the number of schools, which varied the amount of salary each year, averaging about $1,100; re-elected June, 1884. W. J. Cramer, elected June, 1887; salary, $1,500. Superintendent Cramer died on January 23, 1888, and J. W. Leech was appointed and commissioned to fill the unexpired term. J. W. Leech was elected and commissioned June, 1890; salary, $1,500; re-elected June, 1893; salary, $1,700. T. L. Gibson, elected and commissioned June, 1896; salary, $1,-700; re-elected June, 1899; salary, $1,700.

It will be seen from the above record that Mr. McCormick served as county superintendent for five years. The services rendered by him in this office were important and valuable. Other superintendents have done good work, but he was virtually the pioneer in a position of great opportunities and of great responsibility. He was industrious, enthusiastic, tactful, and capable. It was his lot not only to popularize his own office and its authority but the common school system itself. To accomplish these results he visited every school district in the county and became personally acquainted with directors and taxpayers as well as teachers;

he visited the schools and made interesting speeches to the children; his oral examinations of applicants for teachers' certificates were always fair and were held in nearly every town and township in the county and in the presence of citizens and taxpayers. He thus demonstrated the usefulness of his office. He inspired others with his own enthusiasm. He encouraged the holding of school exhibitions in every school district and he personally attended most of them. These exhibitions, which usually took place in the spring of the year, joined to his personal participation in them, had a marvelous effect in creating and sustaining an interest in common schools in Cambria county. Taxes for their support were more freely paid, better methods of instruction were introduced, better teachers were employed, better school-houses were built, and a healthier tone pervaded all educational conditions. Mr. McCormick's term of office expired just as the mutterings of civil strife came up from the South, and there was subsequently much demoralization in the administration of the schools of Cambria county, as elsewhere, but this demoralization did not long continue. Mr. McCormick's good work was not lost.

In a letter which I have recently received from Mr. McCormick he writes that he still does some literary work and that not long ago he contributed to a local newspaper a series of twelve articles on his favorite science of astronomy. Two children and several grandchildren are either with him or are not far away. A married daughter, Lenore, now lives in Germantown, Pennsylvania.

Mr. McCormick died on May 1, 1903, at Oakdale, Stanislaus county, California, and was buried in the Union cemetery at that place. He was 85 years, 10 months, and 13 days old—a good old age.

A REMINISCENCE OF PRESIDENT TAYLOR.

FROM THE BULLETIN OF THE AMERICAN IRON AND STEEL
ASSOCIATION, JUNE 15, 1909.

ZACHARY TAYLOR, the twelfth President of the United
States, occupied this position from the day of his inaugu-
ration on March 5, 1849, until his death on July 9, 1850. In
August, 1849, just sixty years ago, accompanied by a small
party of prominent gentlemen, he journeyed in a carriage
over the turnpikes of that day from Washington to Pittsburgh, thence visiting a few other interior cities before returning to Washington. His carriage route through Pennsylvania embraced Bedford, Somerset, Westmoreland, and Allegheny counties and the towns of Bedford, Somerset, Ligonier, and Greensburg. The President's itinerary was duly
announced several days in advance, and of course excited
much interest. The countryside was on tiptoe to see the
hero of Palo Alto, Resaca de la Palma, Monterey, and
Buena Vista.

The editor of the *Bulletin* was at that time one of the
enthusiastic young Whigs of Johnstown. Learning that the
President and his party would be at Ligonier on a certain
day and would stop there for dinner we induced two of
our friends, boys of about our own age, to go with us to
Ligonier and see the President. Now Ligonier was twenty
miles away, and the only way to get there was on horseback over a mountain road, and if we were to see the President before dinner it was necessary that we should make an
early start. So we started before daylight, three enthusiastic boys, and about 10 o'clock we were in Ligonier, to which
historic town many neighboring farmers had preceded us
on the same mission. Introducing ourselves to Mr. Mendell,
the landlord of the leading public house in the place, we
were most hospitably received. He was surprised to learn
that we had ridden so far. In less than an hour the car-

riages of the Presidential party were seen approaching in a cloud of dust and in a few minutes we boys first saw a President of the United States and one of our country's greatest soldiers.

Preparations for dinner were soon made for the distinguished guests, who were informally welcomed by Mr. Mendell, John Bell, a local ironmaster, and others. When dinner was about to be served we boys obtained a view of the dining room, which would seat about thirty and certainly not more than forty guests at one long table, but we did not think that we could sit at that table until the Presidential party and the local dignitaries had first been served. We were greatly surprised, therefore, when Mr. Mendell came to us and said that boys who had risen so early and ridden so far to see General Taylor should sit at the same table with him. And we did. Mr. Bell sat at the head of the table, the President on his right, and we boys not quite half way down the table on Mr. Bell's left.

After dinner General Taylor was induced to mount a chair in a corner of the parlor of the Mendell House and make an address to all who could crowd inside or hear him through the open windows. Soon afterwards the Presidential party took its departure from Ligonier and we boys started homeward. That incident in our lives when we dined with President Taylor occurred just sixty years ago. There can not be many persons now living who can say that they dined with General Taylor that long ago.

JOHN FRITZ, IRONMASTER.

READ AT THE DINNER TO MR. FRITZ, ON NOVEMBER 17, 1910, BY THE MANUFACTURERS OF PHILADELPHIA.

MY acquaintance with Mr. Fritz began in 1855, fifty-five years ago, when he came to Johnstown as the general superintendent of the Cambria Iron Works, which had been leased on May 15 of that year for a term of five years by the firm of Wood, Morrell & Co. These works had been built in 1853 and 1854 by the Cambria Iron Company as an iron rail mill, with several blast furnaces. They made their first rail on July 27, 1854. Only iron rails were made in this country for several years afterwards. The lease was extended in 1860 for one year and terminated in 1861.

A great problem confronted Mr. Fritz. He had to so manage the works as to make them a financial as well as a mechanical success. He succeeded in both undertakings. In 1856, the year following his assumption of this difficult task, the Cambria Iron Works rolled 13,206 tons of rails, and their annual production was thereafter increased under Mr. Fritz's management. The production in 1856 was only 5,386 tons less than the largest production of any rail mill in the country in that year—the mill of the Phœnix Iron Company rolling 18,592 tons. Those were the days of comparatively small outputs at iron and steel works.

When Mr. Fritz took charge of the Cambria Iron Works he soon discovered that good rails could not be made from pig iron that had been made entirely from Cambria ores; so, after much tribulation, he introduced a mixture of Cambria and other pig iron which worked well and produced good results.

But Mr. Fritz was not satisfied with the results he was accomplishing. The Cambria rail mill was equipped with two-high rolls, and as these could not be operated as satisfactorily as was desirable, and besides often invited accidents, Mr. Fritz conceived the idea of introducing three-high rolls, which had never before been used in any country in the manufacture of rails. This was done, and on July 3, 1857, the innovation proved to be a great success. Mr. Fritz had conspicuously shown his skill as an engineer. Soon there were three-high trains of rolls in all the rail mills of the country.

But a great trial came to Mr. Fritz the day after his successful use of three-high rolls. On July 4 the Cambria Iron Works burned down. We well remember that catastrophe. All but the stoutest hearts were appalled. But Mr. Fritz was equal to the emergency. He infused courage into the breasts of all his men, and at once began the work of clearing away the débris and rebuilding the works. In precisely four weeks the new works were running, and they made 30,000 tons of rails before any interruption occurred from any cause whatever.

Mr. Fritz was surrounded at Johnstown by a remarkably bright collection of engineers and mechanics, all young men, who gave him loyal support but who also learned much from him. They were long known as John Fritz's "boys." We can mention only a few of them: Jacob M. Campbell, Alexander Hamilton, George Fritz, William R. Jones, Daniel N. Jones, William Canam, James Bell, and Thomas H. Lapsley. They are all gone. Robert W. Hunt, the first chemist of the Cambria Iron Works, who is with us to-night, came to Johnstown just as Mr. Fritz left for Bethlehem.

Mr. Fritz's connection with the Cambria Iron Works continued until July, 1860, when he resigned to superintend the erection and operation of the Bethlehem Iron Works, to embrace a number of blast furnaces and a rolling mill to roll iron rails. The rolling mill was successfully started in 1863. In 1873 Mr. Fritz introduced at these works the manufacture of Bessemer steel and Bessemer steel rails, and in 1890 he made for the Navy Department at the works of the Bethlehem Steel Company the first heavy armor plate that had ever been made in this country. The armor plate plant of this company had been built under Mr. Fritz's direction.

A few years ago Mr. Fritz retired from all active participation in the management of iron and steel works, after more than fifty years of unbroken success, which success has brought him many honors. Included in these honors we may mention honorary membership in the British Iron and Steel Institute, which has conferred upon Mr. Fritz the Bessemer gold medal. We may also mention a magnificent banquet which was tendered to Mr. Fritz by a large number of prominent engineers and iron and steel manufacturers at the Waldorf-Astoria in New York in October, 1902, in celebration of his 80th birthday anniversary.

But we feel sure that no honor that has ever come to Mr. Fritz has given him more heartfelt pleasure than the testimonial which he received at Johnstown on July 4, 1860, immediately prior to his departure for his new field of labor at Bethlehem. On that day a superb set of silverware was presented to Mr. Fritz at the rolling mill of the Cambria Iron Works by the employés of Wood, Morrell & Co. Between 1,500 and 2,000 persons were present at the presentation, including many ladies. The presence of this army of workmen and citizens testified to the esteem in which Mr. Fritz was held by the whole community. The set of silverware included a remarkably handsome water pitcher. On it were inscribed these words : " To John Fritz, Esq., General Superintendent of the Cambria Iron Works, as a Testimonial, by the Employees. July 4, 1860." This pitcher was exhibited at the New York crystal palace during the World's Fair in 1853, and it took the first premium as the finest piece of silverware among many specimens that had been collected from all parts of the world. Several addresses were delivered, Mr. Fritz thanking the donors, as the *Cambria Tribune* said, "in a very feeling, frank, and earnest speech."

The *Tribune* devoted much space to an account of the testimonial to Mr. Fritz, remarking at the close of the account that "the gift is but properly in keeping with the measure of the man," and that "in Mr. Fritz the company and this community lose a man and citizen whose place is not easily filled." Mr. Fritz was then 38 years old. He had been general superintendent of the Cambria Iron Works for five years. He was succeeded by his brother, George Fritz.

There is one trait in Mr. Fritz's character which does him especial honor—his readiness on all occasions to give credit to the thousands of men subject to his orders who have contributed by their skill and loyalty to his remarkable success. In an address by Mr. Fritz on the 75th anniversary of the Franklin Institute of Philadelphia on October 4, 1899, he said: "Here I wish to say that I should commit an act of ingratitude should I fail to give credit to the brave and noble workmen who throughout my long connection with the business have ever stood ready to meet any emergency, no matter what the danger or difficulty might be. For the kind and generous manner in which I was always treated by them they ever have a green spot in my memory." This is a gracious compliment from Mr. Fritz to his old companions in many a bitter struggle with engineering and mechanical problems that tested the skill and manhood of all of them, and it is most gracefully expressed.

In the same address, embodying a note of strenuous personal experience, Mr. Fritz also said: "How little do the younger men who have charge of the great iron and steel industries know or even think of the severe mental strain, the great amount of bodily labor, the vexation, the surprises, and the disappointments that the men in charge experienced during the perfecting and erection of these vast establishments that are now engaged in the manufacture of iron and steel."

We are all glad to see Mr. Fritz looking so well tonight. He has hosts of absent friends who would share this pleasure if they were here.* I know of no man in the iron trade who has been so universally respected and loved as John Fritz. His personal qualities have been as lovable as his engineering achievements have been notable.

---

* In a letter to the president of the Manufacturers' Club expressing his regret that he could not participate in the testimonial to his old friend Mr. Carnegie said: "Pray convey to dear Uncle John my warmest regards and congratulations upon his honored old age. Many are the men who on this occasion would join in giving three cheers for Uncle John! I am sure he has not an enemy in the world and he has given to all of us a noble example."

A LESSON FROM THE JOHNSTOWN FLOOD.

WRITTEN IN JUNE, 1889, AFTER WITNESSING THE DESTRUC-
TION CAUSED BY THE FLOOD OF MAY 31.

In the world we live in and in the universe of which
it forms a part there are many evidences of a stupendous
plan, as was long ago demonstrated by philosophical writers.
The sun is set in the heavens; the planets revolve in their
orbits; the earth turns on its axis; the seasons come and
go; the sea ebbs and flows. The doctrine of evolution may
to some minds account for physical growth and development, but it fails to account for the existence of a *plan* in
the creation of the universe.

A *plan* logically implies a *planner,* as has also been
pointed out by philosophical writers.

Not only are there evidences of a grand *plan* which
must have had a *planner,* but there are evidences without
number of the existence of immutable *laws* for the government of the universe. The sun is not only set in the
heavens but it gives forth heat and light with unfailing
regularity; the planets revolve in their orbits, through millions and millions of miles of space, with such precision
that their coming and going and their positions toward one
another may be calculated with mathematical exactness;
the earth not only turns on its axis but it turns so exactly
that from day to day and from year to year there is
not the variation of a second of time in its revolutions; the
seasons come and go in regular order; the proud waves of
the tempestuous seas are stayed by unchanging boundaries.

We can not conceive of the existence of immutable
laws without conceding the existence of a *law-maker.*

We have, then, in one person or essence, a *planner,* or
creator, and a *law-maker.* Is it reasonable to suppose that
the creator of the universe and the maker of the laws
which govern it should cease to *control* the work of his

own hands ? Certainly not. Therefore he *rules;* he is the great *ruler*.

If the *planner* of the universe, the *maker* of its laws, and the *administrator* of these laws be one and the same person, or essence, it must necessarily follow that whatever he doeth he doeth *well*. He would not do ill with *his own handiwork*. The planets do not crash into one another, nor does the sun fail to give heat and light, or the earth fail to produce food for man and beast. He would not do ill with *his own creatures*. Is it conceivable, therefore, that the creator and ruler of the universe and the author of our existence should punish us after death because we had been weak when we should have been strong, or because, like Bartimeus of old, we were blind and could not see the way ? Is not our punishment on earth enough ? We suffer in the flesh and with mental agony for violations of the great creator's laws by ourselves or by those who have gone before us, and death itself, the common lot, is a great terror, from which we would all escape if we could.

The inborn hope of immortality, the promises of the New Testament, and the precepts and example of the Founder of Christianity, whether he be accepted as the Son of God or as the greatest of all the teachers and prophets, are incentives to all men to lead upright and useful lives and to prove themselves in all things worthy of the divinity that is within them. No wise man will undervalue these influences; they have made the human race all that it is to-day. But that the poor creature who was born with vicious and criminal instincts, or who became both vicious and criminal through the influence of evil surroundings which he had not chosen, is to be punished after death is a doctrine which rests for acceptance solely upon the theory that the creator and the ruler of the universe and the author of our being is a vindictive God. But vindictiveness is not an attribute of the Almighty, while mercy is. Surely infinite mercy can not be less merciful than the evenhanded justice of this world, which imposes only penalties that are commensurate with the offenses against which they are directed. Punishment after death, added to the punishment of death itself, would bear no just relation to

even the gravest of earthly offenses. Who can sound the
deepest depths of even a murderer's temptation, or accu-
rately measure the inherited defects of his physical and
mental and moral nature?

The Ten Commandments contain no hint of either rewards or punishments after death. The punishments of
the Old Testament are distinctly of this world; nor does
the Old Testament anywhere so far as we have observed
speak of rewards to the righteous after death. In the Fifth
Commandment we are told to "honor thy father and thy
mother"—for what reason?—"that thy days may be long
upon the land which the Lord thy God giveth thee."

The doctrine of a future state of rewards and punishments can not be inferred from the Old Testament accounts of the death and burial of the patriarchs, kings, and
prophets. "Abraham gave up the ghost and died in a good
old age, an old man, and full of years, and was gathered
to his people." "And Isaac gave up the ghost and died
and was gathered to his people, being old and full of days."
"And when Jacob had made an end of commanding his
sons he yielded up the ghost and was gathered unto his
people." "Now the days of David drew nigh that he
should die, and he charged Solomon, his son, saying I go
the way of all the earth. So David slept with his fathers."
In these and other Old Testament accounts the dying express no hope of future reward or fear of future punishment. Indeed they say nothing about a future state.

In the Lord's Prayer every Christian child is given
lasting impressions of a Heavenly Father which are loving,
soothing, and strengthening. "Deliver us from evil" does
not even hint of punishment after death as an evil from
which we ask to be delivered. Why should the spirit of
this prayer ever be departed from by those who teach us
more of this Heavenly Father than our Saviour himself
has taught us in its simple words and in many other ex-
amples and precepts which he has set before us and com-
mended to our hearts?

If it shall be answered that there are passages in the
Old and the New Testaments, but particularly in the New
Testament, which are in conflict with the above views

of God's justice and mercy, and which appear to confirm the doctrine of future punishment, we ask the reader to consider that these passages have been variously interpreted by conscientious and scholarly Bible students, and that they should be read in connection with other passages which clearly set forth God's love for his children and not apart from them. Many statements in both the Old and the New Testament are now generally discredited by reverent Bible critics; why not also those statements which are not in harmony with our conception of the Great Creator as our Heavenly Father? Even the Sermon on the Mount is not free from criticism by reverent Bible students.

We have been led into this train of thought by the contemplation of the awful calamity which has just swept nearly 2,500 persons from time into eternity, in the twinkling of an eye and without a moment's warning that they had reached the end of all earthly things. Shall it be said that these innocent victims of man's violation of nature's laws must be punished hereafter? The very thought is abhorrent to our sense of infinite justice and mercy.

We have also since the flood been impressed by the reflection that among all our acquaintances and in all our reading and in all the sermons to which we have listened we have never heard of a man or woman of evangelical faith who was willing to admit that any of his or her deceased relatives had been consigned to a state of future punishment, no matter how grave their offenses may have been. Apparently all men and all women have faith in the exemption from future punishment of their own friends. The human heart will not condemn its own. Are the affectionate impulses of the human heart to be ignored? Is the logic of its love for its own to count for nothing? What else is the inborn hope of immortality but a trusting faith in the existence of a state of future happiness, adapted, it may be, to our individual capacity to enjoy it? The hope of immortality, if interpreted in a spirit of Christian charity, implies freedom from future punishment for all men, and does not embody the selfish belief that a privileged few, as a special favor, may escape from its awful infliction upon their own persons.

FULLNAME INDEX

LINTON (cont.)
  Mary 57 59 Mr 62 Mrs 59
  63 Phoebe 59 Robert P 62
  Robert Park 59 William 57
LINTONS, & Galbreath 62 65
LIVERMORE, Pamilla 36
LONG, Diebold 99 Elizabeth
  99 Jacob 99 Oswald 99
LOVELL, Mr 78 Mrs 78
LOWER, Susan 76
LYTLE, Robert 115
MACLAY, William I 56
MAGEHAN, James 58
  Michael Dan 81-82 117-118
MAGUIRE, T A 96 Thomas A
  11 127
MARSHALL, 125
MARTIN, Morrell & Co 72 Mr
  73 Oliver 72
MATTHEWS, John 59 Mary
  59
MCCLANE, John 35 Julia 35
MCCLELLAN, 87
MCCONNELL, A D 125
MCCORMICK, Andrew 124-
  125 Ann 124 Eliza 125
  John 124 Lenore 128 Mr
  126 128 S B 125 127
  William C 80 Winfield Scott
  126
MCCREARY, Elizabeth 36
MCCULLOUGH, Hannah 96
MCDONALD, Joseph 61 93
  117
MCDONALDS, 123
MCFARREN, Samuel 33
MCGEE, Charles 27
MCKEE, Elizabeth 36 Jane 31
  35 Margaret 36
MCKINNEY, Peter 95
MCMICHAEL, Morton 75 121
MCNEAL, Hugh 65

MENDELL, Mr 129-130
MERRIMAN, George 62
MILESE, John G 117
MILLER, D M 34
MITCHELL, Foster W 121
MOORE, Johnston 123
  Martha 36 Miss 85 Silas 60
MORRELL, Daniel 72 Daniel
  J 121 Daniel Johnson 71
  David 71-72 Mr 73-76
  Susan 76 Susannah 71
  Thaddeus 71
MORRISON, Abraham 12
MUDD, Rebecca G 79
MULLIGAN, Col 111
MULLIN, 82 & Albright 116
  Alexander C 81 Alexander
  Chesterfield 114 Catharine
  114 Emma Matilda 116
  George 114 Mr 116-123
MUNSON, George W 41
MURRAY, Charles D 117
  George 115
MYERS, Jacob 61
NELSON, Agnes 77
NEWELL, Rebecca 96
NOONS, 123
OGLE, Emily 46
ORR, William 84
OSBORN, Matthew 124
OTT, William M 122
PACKER, Asa 121
PARK, Ann 57 60 63 Elizabeth
  57 John 57 63 Mary 57
  Robert 57
PARKS, Mary A 30
PATTERSON, Dr 37 R H 37
  Robert 75 Robert M 64
PENN, William 53
PERSHING, Christopher 99
  Cyrus 100 Cyrus L 29 37
  41 44 56 92 99 102 103 106